HALO-HALO

HALO-HALO

A POETIC MIX OF HISTORY,
CULTURE, IDENTITY, REVELATION,
AND REVOLUTION

JUSTINE S. RAMOS

NEW DEGREE PRESS

HALO-HALO

A poetic mix of history, culture, identity, revelation, and revolution

ISBN   978-1-63676-911-0 *Paperback*

              978-1-63676-975-2 *Kindle Ebook*

              978-1-63730-079-4 *Ebook*

"I have the ability to make that white man know I am just as mean as anybody in this world ... I could make him think, and I could make them recognize that I'm a mean son of a bitch in terms of my direction fighting for the rights of Filipinos in this country. Because I feel we are just as good as any of them. I feel we have the same rights as any of them. Because in that Constitution, it said that everybody has equal rights and justice. You've got to make that come about. They are not going to give it to you."

—*LARRY ITLIONG*

CONTENTS

———

Dedicated to:

*the Black, brown, and Indigenous activists who fight
tirelessly. Your work will not go down in vain.*

*those who have informed, educated, and empowered me to
stand my ground, to speak louder, and to stand taller.*

those who have fallen unjustly.

immigrants, dreamers, and fighters.

*my family, for never letting me forget a language
that could've rolled off my tongue and a culture that
could've withered away from my memory.*

*my brother, who will probably pretend to
read my book from start to end.*

Rustlypoo, the best, fluffiest friend in the world.

AUTHOR'S NOTE

My *Ninang* (godmother) rushes me out of our creaky twin-sized bed at 5am. She swiftly throws on her secondhand scrubs and puts me in a mismatched outfit. We skip breakfast and make our way down our apartment. She pulls my arm as we run across the street to get to the Metro bus. My small four-year-old legs cannot not keep up with her. *"Dali na! Aalis na yung bus. Malalate tayo!"* "Hurry up! The bus is leaving. We're going to be late!"

Much to our dismay, the bus zooms off right as we make our way to the stop. We plop down on the cold metal bench and look at each other with jaded eyes.

I let out a sigh and am fascinated with the cool cloud that escapes my mouth. Things like that don't happen in the Philippines, but it's a common occurrence on chilly Los Angeles mornings. My Ninang looks at her watch anxiously and opens a brochure of the bus timetable.

"Hirap buhay 'Merica." "Life's hard in America," I tell Ninang.

She chuckles at first but looks at me with a hint of sadness in her eyes.

"Mahirap nga, Anak. Kung na sa Pinas tayo, tulog pa tayo sana noh?" "It is hard, my child. If we were in the Philippines we'd still be sleeping, huh?" She smiles softly.

We would go on to repeat the phrase *"Hirap buhay 'Merica"* a thousand times more after this instance. From accompanying my mom from one caregiving job to another, to hiding in closets from non-child friendly patients, to escaping through back windows when patients became deranged, to shuffling through books in thrift shops and trying to scrape thick accents off my tongue, *"Hirap buhay 'Merica"* is just a short way of encapsulating immigrant life.

Beyond the romanticized and idealized vision of the United States many Pilipinx people dream of are stories of immigrant struggle and plight. Under the ideas of wealth and dreams are stories of sleepless nights and tireless mornings. Beyond the notions of welcome and opportunity are moments of isolation, loneliness, and alienation. There's pressure to succeed and provide for family back home. For my parents and many other immigrant families, there's anxiety about keeping your family happy and alive. For the children of the diaspora, it's figuring out belonging, identity, and home. It's trying to be the fruit of your parents' labor in a foreign land not made for you to thrive in. I struggled to understand the layers of my identity and self. I was born in the Philippines, raised with strong Philippine values, but put into a world that rejects all of the values I was taught. I wanted to hold on to my native tongue, but my school insisted I let it go. I was so proud of my native cuisine, but my peers thought it should stay at home.

In fact, I remember having to do a project on our favorite dessert in the fourth grade. While my peers presented their grandmother's sixty-year-old chocolate chip cookie recipe or Marie Callender's banana cream pie, I presented on *halo-halo*—a cup of colorful, nostalgic happiness filled with shaved ice, evaporated milk, ube jam, jackfruit, nata de coco, and so much more. I remember being so excited to show off something so special and unique to my identity and background, only for my classmates to laugh and make disgusted faces during my presentation.

Suddenly, I didn't want to be Pilipinx anymore. I felt ashamed of where I was born, how I was raised, and who I was. My cultural identity became this huge secret I kept just to avoid being bullied. It got to a point where I began to let others define my identity for me. When people assumed I was Chinese, I just smiled approvingly. When people assumed I was Latinx, I pursed my lips and nodded. When people thought I was biracial, I just accepted and agreed. I didn't bother to correct people or take pride in my roots because whenever I did, all I received was ridicule and disgust. And when you spend years letting other people define who you are, you lose a sense of yourself.

I would spend my years after trying to deconstruct and comprehend my experiences and identity through poetry, specifically slam poetry. I actively competed with a youth spoken word organization called Get Lit – Words Ignite and became closely involved with all of its members. I then moved on to mentorship and coaching in the spoken word realm and fostered the creativity of the youth. I joined the organization WriteGirl as both a mentee and a mentor, and received my first poetry publication in their anthology, *Sound Generation.* I would also go on to win awards from the Youth Poet Laureate Association and became published in Teen Ink National Literary Magazine, Power Poetry, and Cornell University's *Rainy Day Literary Magazine.*

Despite my love for poetry, I realized I never once wrote a poem about my identity and culture. In trying to understand my experiences, I left out a large chunk of my identity simply because I felt unqualified to even talk about it. I felt like an imposter in my own community despite being born in the Philippines, being Pilipinx, and being raised with strong Philippine values.

It wasn't until later, in my undergraduate years at UCLA, where I began to indulge in Philippine history and surround myself with fellow Pilipinx youth and other children of the diaspora. I realized I was not alone in my experiences. These feelings of imposter syndrome within my own culture are a shared experience. Immigrant plight and struggle is a shared experience. Navigating through higher education as a first-generation student is a shared experience. *"Hirap Buhay 'Merica"* is a shared experience.

I learned about the hundreds of years of Philippine colonization and violence––from Spain, to Japan, to the United States and China. I learned about Pilipinx feminists, leaders, rebels, revolutionaries, activists, and scholars. I learned about Pilipinx-American farmworkers, union leaders, writers, academics, and leaders. I shared similar stories and experiences with my peers who accepted me. We all bonded over the nostalgia of our Pilipinx childhood and upbringing. We discussed Philippine politics and the state of Pilipinx-Americans in the United States. We all expressed our frustration with the lack of Pilipinx representation and discourse. We all vowed to represent our culture in any way that we could. We disseminated the usage of the word "Pilipinx" versus "Pilipino." Most importantly, we all enjoyed the same kind of food, and nobody had to worry about laughs or disgusted faces.

I remember introducing halo-halo to my friend. I explained that it translated into "mix-mix" and is typically made with various components from the munggo beans, the jackfruit, the leche flan, the nata de coco, and the ube jam. My friend asked me about the origins of some of these ingredients, most of which did not directly come from the Philippines. It was in the midst of my explanation when I realized that a dessert I knew to be fully and undoubtedly Pilipino had mixed roots and origins in itself. The leche flan from Spain, the canned evaporated milk from the United States, the munggo beans from Japan, and so on. Despite these mixed origins, I still upheld halo-halo as the most Pilipino dessert I could imagine.

I realized I've been gatekeeping myself from my own culture and identity because I felt I lacked authenticity. I felt like I wasn't Pilipinx enough. Yet, here's a cup of halo-halo, with "mix-mix" roots, swirling in colorful shades of Pilipino pride.

I realized being Pilipinx or Pilipinx-American is a lot like a halo-halo. We are complex, multicultural, and multilayered individuals with history that collides with Spain, Japan, the United States, and so on. Layers of colonization and the flight of the diaspora may have confused and scattered us, but we still ended up together in this beautiful, complex mix of a culture and community. We are an amalgam of history, culture, revolution and poetry, and I could not be prouder to be undoubtedly Pilipinx.

My poetry is dedicated to all the textbooks that left my country and culture out of the narrative. My poetry is devoted to anyone who has ever uttered *"Hirap Buhay 'Merica"* under their breath. My poetry is for all of the beautiful immigrants, first-generation students, dreamers, activists, and creatives who have given life to each word in this book.

As you turn the page, you'll read snippets of frustrations and reflections. You'll read flashes of my childhood, a peek into the crevices of my heart and memory. You'll hear outrage, hope, and a desperate call for advocacy and awareness. These pages contain the tears of those who have lost a sense of themselves, those who have let the world define who they are, and the strength of those who, like me, are on the journey of finding themselves again.

Turn the page and you'll hear the squeak of a twin-sized bed and small four-year-old feet, running, running, running toward her dreams of not missing the bus headed toward self-revelation.

(P.S.: I know Philippine history and culture is not familiar to all. I know some of the poetic structures I use--particularly Golden Shovels and acrostics--may not be something you learned in your lifetime. I have provided notes at the end of the book that explain ideas, themes, figures, or events of poems. These notes, however, should not be the end of your learning or perhaps unlearning. I invite you to dive deeper into subjects that pique your curiosity.)

(P.S.S: Golden Shovel Poems—The Golden Shovel is a poetic form created by Terrance Hayes to pay homage to Gwendolyn Brooks. The Golden Shovel takes a favored line or favored lines from an existing poem and uses them as the last word of each line in an entirely new poem. Due to the layout of pages in this book, the Golden Shovel and Acrostic forms were not completely retained. Modified adjustments were made. Acrostic—a poem in which the first letters of each line spell out a word or phrase.)

CHAPTER 1

HISTORY

———

Holding textbooks that discuss your people in present tense
is a privilege many don't get to know. It's up to us to
search for memories erased, buried, lost in the
trenches of colonialism.
Our people deserve to know their stories. The future must
remember how we survived and continue to thrive.
You wield the power to author your story, to write
   unwritten histories.

Ferdinand Magellan

The teacher says, "Ferdinand Magellan lead the first
expedition to circumnavigate the globe,
he couldn't finish it because he was killed b*y savages* in
the Philippines"

Then,
Eyes burn holes through my spine
the flame flickers between each foramen,
carves *shame* across my skin

I don't look up, I don't look back
Instead, I rub my thumb across a map of a
familiar archipelago,
a 3x3 picture under the portrait of Magellan,
back and forth as if the strokes of my finger could
teleport me back home where I can
feel the cool mush of rice fields under my feet,
grains of salty sand and sea between my toes
as if I could float along the Santa Maria River on my back
extinguishing the flames that simmer my bones,
ignited by the arsonists in my classroom who
keep pulling the trigger on their flamethrower eyes
screaming *you* did this

The teacher holds me hostage under his gaze: *Can you tell
us more about Lapu-Lapu?*

The flames turn into ice and suddenly
I have brain freeze
my voice is stuck in an ice cube I cannot swallow down
I look at a 2x2 picture of a man half-clothed, holding
a *Kampilan,*
a man who looks like my family but alas,
a man who I don't know.
I shake my head
I don't look up, I don't look back

Somehow, this is worse than the flames.
Not knowing who your people are or
how to defend them from arsonists who keep
burning pages of my culture's history that
I didn't get to read
pages that nobody will get to read
pages turned into ash, turned into ink to
write a history book like this.

Written by some man who doesn't look like my family
some man who I don't know
some man who nobody in the archipelago seems to know
some man who has probably never step foot in mushy rice
fields or
dipped their toes in our warm, salty oceans and sands
who doesn't know how it feels for the sun to toast his
stomach while
 floating in the Santa Maria River
some man who shrunk portraits of your heroes into
minuscule flashcards
printed with the very ink made from the ashes of my
history

I rub my thumb across the pictures over and over,
as if they'll come alive and tell me who they are
how they've been, what their truth is, how to defend them,
how to grow a spine and how to
melt my ice-cubed voice into liquid honey to
put out the flames in my back.

But I stay frozen in place,
my spine slowly cremates against the fire,
I don't look up. I don't look back.

This is how it feels to not know my history,
to not know myself.

Golden Shovel: Rizal

Kabataan ang pag-asa ng bayan
The youth is the hope of our future

—*JOSE RIZAL*[1]

When Mother Earth's heart quakes as **the**
conquerors uproot Her mountains and stain
Her waters with blood, it's the **youth**
who tend to Her shores and embrace Her roots.
Cleaning up the mess of past generations **is**
a job they were assigned to as soon as their toes
hugged the soil and listened to **the**
Earth's shaky weeps from under their feet.
They paint Her skies in watercolor shades of **hope**
covering up dewdrop tears, turned into pounding
rivers. Wiping her cheeks **of**
all that was burned and conquered. The youth are **our**
gardeners who have the burden of planting seeds
to turn into trees, then forests in the **future**

---

1   Toshinao Urabe, "Remarks of Ambassador Toshinao Urabe 38th Ship
     for Southeast Asian Youth Programme (SSEAYP)" Embassy of Japan in
     the Philippines, accessed November 10, 2020.

Golden Shovel: Andrés Bonifacio

"Aling pag-ibig pa ang hihigit kaya
sa pagkadalisay at pagkadakila
gaya ng pag-ibig sa tinubuang lupa?
Alin pag-ibig pa? Wala na nga, wala."

"PAG-IBIG SA TINUBUANG LUPA," ANDRÉS BONIFACIO[2]

"Is there any love that is nobler purer and more
sublime than the love of the native country?
What love is? Certainly none.

"PAG-IBIG SA TINUBUANG LUPA,"

TRANSLATED BY EPIFANIO DELOS SANTOS

When you are extracted from the soil that
nourished your soul, there **is**
no way you can plant yourself in another land where **there**
isn't warm water or where the sun doesn't
drip golden dew, where there aren't **any**
sunshine-stroked hands to pamper you with all their **love.**
The farmers say **that**
displacing a tree, no matter how young, **is**
harmful to the future fruits of its labor and though
some may find it **nobler**
to find a home that is supposedly more beautiful,
there is nothing **purer**
than to grow where you are originally planted **and**
bask in the beauty of your birth, where there are **more**
familiar faces and hands. Where the oceans are **sublime**

---

2   "Andres Bonifacio's 'Pag-Ibig sa Tinubuang Lupa," National Government
Portal, accessed November 26, 2020.

and where the hillsides are greener **than**
this land of transplants, where **the**
hands who hold you, don't seem to do it with **love.**
Still, you spend years battling stunted growth
in this land **of**
unfamiliar hands and faces, so you begin to wonder about **the**
parts of yourself left in your **native**
soil, and you think, what if I was meant to
grow in my true **country?**
This world has told you to bloom where you
are planted, but **what**
if you cannot flower without the genuine **love**
of your people? Then they ask, if this New Land isn't
enough for you, then what **is?**
and you respond: this New Land is **certainly**
not my Homeland, and if I can't choose my
native soil, I'd rather choose **none.**

4 July 1776

Give me liberty
or give me death,[3]
Wave that banner and
play the songs of freedom---
This land is not your land, this land is *my* land
Red splatters in the air
after the lash of a whip
The Birth of our Nation is painted White
To mask Black lips that turn Blue

How does it feel to live in the Land of the Free?
Sing--This land's made for you,[4]

not me.

---

3   Patrick Henry, "Speech to the Second Virginia Convention" (speech, St. John's Church, March 23, 1775).

4   Woodie Guthrie and the US Coast Guard Band, "This Land is Your Land," The Library of Congress, February 1940.

4 July 1902[5]

Freedom can be bought with the price of a luxury yacht[6]

Surrender the Brown to the White
hold their necks, paint their faces Red
pinch their jugulars until their lips turn Blue
Convince them their irises should be the same shade too

Refuse to acknowledge defeat because
Brown can never stand alone
Unless it is 200,000 Brown bodies
laying cold and limp in their homes

A genocide in April: Imperial Mission complete

A celebration in July: You're no longer free

---

5   Becky Little, "The Surprising Connection Between the Philippines and
    the Fourth of July," National Geographic, accessed July 1, 2020.
6   The Philippines was bought for $20 million by the United States from
    Spain on July 4, 1992.

4 July 1946[7]

If we cannot have your land,
We'll force you to remember it was once ours

We'll exit your building
but keep one foot in the door,
Stretching our toes inside Military Bases,
digging our heels in metal bullets, and
packing gun powder beneath our nails

Kick the backs of Pilipino children so hard
they forget their Native language,
Feed them spoonfuls of Alphabet Soup, sourced from
the *American English Dictionary,*
tell them they are Independent,
but cannot survive without *US*

Call it Filipino-American Friendship Day
and maybe they'll forget about the war
maybe they'll forget about the 200,000
and who they should be fighting for

---

7   "Republic Day," Official Gazette, accessed July 4, 2020.
(July 4, 1946 is the day the United States formally recognized
    the independence of the Republic of the Philippines.)

3 July 2020[8]

Hypocrisy is when the day
that commemorates the silence of voices
and the imprisonment of justice
comes right before the day
that commemorates revolution.

Irony is when a country nourished with the
blood of warriors and activists
who resisted and fought against the
weeds of colonization
becomes afraid of its own roots

An *oxymoron* is when the word a*nti-terror*
is engraved next to pages swearing to murder
those who resist war criminals who sleep peacefully
under pristine, ivory houses built with the bones
of people with slit throats and ghost voices and those
who bathe comfortably in the blood of those
they swore to protect.

---

8   The day Philippine President Rodrigo Duterte signed the anti-terror law.

Maria Lorena Barros

A pen is as powerful as a bullet.
But it is only when we march, shout, and raise our fists
where our words cannot wither away.
They'll be engraved on pages I wrote on and
the minds of people I spoke to

When I leave, my voice will still echo through the soil of
this land and
the throats of the people we fought for.
What we do in our lifetime is not simply erased if
we are not afraid to bleed, shout, and instigate trouble
to make sure our children and grandchildren learn to be
as invincible as us.
I refuse to float in the clouds, look down and be
disappointed that I had to leave
a crumbling city in fear of a ₱35,000 price tag stapled to
my head.

This is not my legacy.

This is our *history*
and the dreams and hopes of our ancestors
who are proud to see us pick up their stories, and mold
them into monuments in our hearts and
memorials in these pages that echo their cries for a
free land, a homeland, one barren of violence from
prayerless dictators. And

finally,
they can rest by the Philippine sea,
sleeping in their peaceful village.

Red

The Smithsonian Museum of American History says:

Red symbolizes hardiness and valor[9]

and the footprints of Indigenous families on jagged trails,
stretching for 5045 miles.
It's the splash of bodies crashing in the Mississippi River
and the palms and necks of white men holding rusty
chains
and ropes, forcing children to tiptoe over the cold bodies
of their mothers and fathers as if they're on a
frail, creaky gangplank, leading their way into endless
waters of blood ribbons and reflections of
stone cold eyes who have seen death too soon.
Perhaps we have confused *survival* for hardiness,
trauma for valor, and Red for violence.

---

9   "The History of the American Flag," *Public Broadcasting Service*, accessed
     January 31, 2021.

White

The Smithsonian Museum of American History says:

White symbolizes purity and innocence[10]

or perhaps, pointed hoods and blood drop crosses
stomping on Yakima, Washington, and then
Wenatchee,
burning neighborhoods where
Tatays and Titos pray the rosary and
kneel to Mama Mary, hoping an
angel could deliver their
voicemail prayers to their families
across the sea.

or maybe it means white women in Watsonville.
Too sacred, Pure, and Innocent to
hold hands or dance with America's *little brown brothers.*[11]
Filipino fingernails form crescents of soil and dreams of
a family in this new-found land but
politicians call them a *menace,*
a threat to the white man's pride and
lighter fluid to the white man's prejudice.

---

10   "The History of the American Flag," *Public Broadcasting Service,* accessed
     January 31, 2021.
11   "The Philippine War—Suppressing an Insurrection," National Park Ser-
     vice, accessed January, 31, 2021.

but really, it means the white man's rage
setting stars and stripes ablaze.
using the Constitution as a club, whacking out
the seeds of *All men are created equal* [12] in the homes of
our Titos and Tatays who are mid-sentence of a Hail Mary,
praying for warm tropical rain and
the sound of church bells
but instead are met with ash fall and
a hurricane of metal shells.

---

12 Thomas Jefferson, "The Declaration of Independence," accessed January
31, 2021.

Blue

The Smithsonian Museum of American History says:

Blue represents vigilance, perseverance and justice[13]

and swollen bruises on the eyes of Black women
whose tears cannot escape the smack of white fists and
the lash of leather whips.

It's the ghostly gasps of children snatched from their
mother's arms,
sold to men in Blue ties with Blue eyes.
It's the shade of moments where Black women realize their
vigilance expires in the dark where pale men crawl inside,
and
spread their thighs,
and nobody can hear their cries, and not even
the fruit flies can testify
what they heard that night,
so they have no choice but to run inside,
persevere and internalize the
pain swelling in their eyes
and hope one day people will rise,
see through the lies, serve justice and finally
hear their bellowing cries

---

13   "The History of the American Flag," *Public Broadcasting Service,* accessed
January 31, 2021.

Ode to the Manongs

They don't call it the grapes of wrath for no reason
feel the wrath of the sun baking into the melanin you were
taught to hate
the wrath of the white man's pocket change thrown in
your face
"This is your worth" he says
The pennies burn the surface of your skin
and melts into the dirt beneath your knees
close your eyes and imagine the humidity of home
quenching your thirst for more
in this country that promised to be a dreamland

Close your eyes and clench your fists
raise them in the air
hold your *hermanos* and *kuyas*
hold your *hermanas* and *atés*
hold them tight and feel
 your shared ancestry coursing through your blood
a community whose history reeks of colonialism and
erasure
but
feel the rhythm of your heart
and clap

Know History, Know Self—Delano, 1965

Kick off your shoes when they tell you to *pull yourself up
by the bootstraps*
Never assume they even tie their own laces.
On September 8, 1965, we finally went barefoot. The soles
of our feet sizzle
Workers--underpaid, overworked,
Hispanics, Latinos, and Pilipinos beaten by the sun, fed
crumbs, paid in dirt
Itliong, Vera Cruz, Huerta, rise and raise signs
yelling *Huelga!*
Singing--*Viva la revolución!*
There's blood on those grapes, this is why wine is red
On the soil and leaves are outlines of teardrops and
memories worth
Remembering, often lifesaving, especially when labor
camp rooms grow lonely
You must remember the Manongs and their fighting spirit

Keep telling their stories and singing the songs of justice
Never forget the unity of our Titos and Tíos, Titas and Tías
On July 1970, we finally won but don't put your shoes back on
We shouldn't stop here. Especially when our Titos and
Tíos, Titas and Tías are
Still beaten by the sun, fed crumbs, paid in dirt--
underpaid, overworked
Ending revolutions is impossible when
Landlords, growers, and money moguls keep punching
holes in your soles,
Forever remember the Manongs, their bouncing picket
signs, voices booming, *Huelga!*

Know History, Know Self—International Hotel, 1968-1977

Kababayans-countrymen squeeze in rooms as big as a
Balikbayan Box.
No room for family; just their hearts and hopes
Of picking up the crumbs of the American Dream, but
they
Wake to the clacking of horses and cops with batons
Human chains of Black, brown and, white shield the
International Home of the Manongs and immigrants who
Shake at the screams of protestors, beaten bloody.
The white shadow of the American Dream
Omits the people who glow in color under its pale light
Remember your place, Chinks, the cops grunt. But the
chain
Yells, *ipaglaban ang I-Hotel!-fight for the I-Hotel!*

*Kung papaalisin tayo, saan tayo pupunta?-If they make us
leave, where do we go?*
Nobody wants us taking space in their blinding spotlight.
Our only option is to open our arms and from the bottom
of our bellies chant:
We won't move. We won't move. We won't move.
Slicing through chains of skin, chants, and blood, horses
stomp on Manongs and
Evict communities that have struggled, laughed, and cried
together for decades.
Lolos-grandfathers limp out of the streetlights into a
coldhearted San Francisco
Finding crumbs of the American Dream in between their
chapped lips that suddenly taste so bitter

Golden Shovel: Dr. Dawn Mabalon

*It is my hope that the love, respect, and commitment we feel
for our historic community runs deeper than anything that
can divide us.* **Little Manila will always be in our hearts.**[14]

—DAWN BOHULANO MABALON,

LITTLE MANILA IS IN THE HEART, 2013

Textbooks know nothing, and our people know too **little**
about the history and stories of those who rebuilt **Manila**
in a hostile land that we now call home. It **will**
only be remembered if we scoop up the sands
of Stockton in our palms and **always**
remember the Manongs and Manangs who built
this town with their hearts and if we can **be**
brave enough to admit our vulnerability and
resiliency as people who have survived **in**
a land that has tried to regurgitate our spirits
and dissolve **our**
dreams and futures. We must remember these
stories and grow this history in our **hearts.**

---

14 Dawn Bohulano Mabalon, *Little Manila is in the Heart* (North Carolina:
Duke University Press, 2013), 1–458.

CHAPTER 2

CULTURE

———

Call your ancestors by embracing their traditions like
    banana leaves on *suman– sticky rice cake.*
Unhook the ropes that strangle your wrists from holding
    the hand of the tropical
land that nourishes your leaves and buds
till they bloom into fluttering sampaguitas, trying to
    survive in cold winds and hard waters.
Understanding your culture begins with
Reclaiming stolen seeds of identity, tucking them into a bed
    of self-love, and watering them till they
Emerge as velvet white petals, stained with the golden dew
    of the Philippine sun.

Irony

There is no greater irony than a culture
who Glorifies, Obsesses, and Desires
the very features of their colonizers

Balikbayan Box

Beneath layers of Halloween chocolate,
under the clearance towels and
cans of Spam
is the heart of a lone star who yearns to go *home*

No, not this home.
This cold, empty one with a rice cooker
made for a lonely stomach and meals for one.
Not this home where I have to turn up the volume of
teleseryes to mimic the music of my village---
the whispers of Titas gossiping
the hearty laughter of Titos chuckling, and
the pitter-patter of little feet running.

Not this home,
deprived of the rustling of
elders sweeping and
the crow of the neighborhood rooster at the
soft stretch of sunlight.

They say home is where the heart is but
what if I haven't found a home here, in this
cold and empty space where the sun
burns skin, where the wind cuts lips,
where the rain gets you sick and
is never warm enough to play in?

What if I left my heart in the Philippine sun
that calls for me to hurry on home?
What if I keep sending Balikbayan Box
after Balikbayan Box
kasi gusto ko bumalik sa bayan ko?
–because I want to go back to my country?

Balikbayan means to *go back home*,
but no matter how much I want to swim across the sea
and carry my heart back to me,
it's planted where my culture is rooted
and it's difficult to uproot a tree that clings
so desperately to the sun's rays who embrace her,
the wind that cradles her
and the warm rain that comforts her

so for now, I will send pieces of myself back home in this
box
in between chocolates,
underneath the towels, and cans
to feed my heart I left with you.
Hanggang sa bumalik ako sa bayan ko
–Until I come back to my country

Hirap Buhay 'Merica

Clouds of frozen breath linger in the air and
whisk away with the smog at the tail of a Metro bus.

My four-year-old lungs pinch me, reminding me to
stop exhaling before I pass out.
But I am too fascinated with my ability to create clouds
with my mouth in the national freezer called America.

In the Philippines, freezers and fridges are a delicacy.
A privilege only known to families who are lucky enough
to have a surplus of food for the next day.

Here, I'm encapsulated in a world of magical ice boxes and
endless ACs
that makes my breath stand against gravity.

Maybe this is why they say that living in America
is paradise,
a privilege you forget exists the longer you are stored in
this frozen wasteland that
holds your identity hostage in mid-air,
soaking in the scarcity of goosebumps and shivers
while your family back home is drenched in the sweat of
the sun

Sarap ng buhay sa America noh?–Life is good in America huh?
Titos and Titas chuckle as our 30-minute calling card ticks
against the clock that
seems to go by faster in America.

There's never enough time in America.

No time to wake up to a bed of fresh *kanin—rice.*
No time to gossip with your neighbors,
much less know their names.
No time to *not work* so we can survive another day
in this endless tundra of frostbite and freezer burns
you're supposed to be grateful for and appreciate
even though your skin yearns to sleep in a pillow of
tropical humidity and bask in the golden rays of the
Philippine sun.

But for now, I wait for an air-conditioned bus that has
sped away, leaving me in its trail of cloudy smog and
frozen sighs with screams of *home* trapped in every crystal.

The bus stop says 5:30, it is only 5:20.
There's never enough time in America,
never fast enough to catch up in America.
You cannot hang on to the tail-end of a *jeepney* or
yell *habol! habol!—chase! chase!* to the drivers in America.

You must wait in the cold,
watch your breath stretch its arms across the Pacific
and when your Titos and Titas call,
Sarap ng buhay sa America noh?
bite your tongue from saying
Hirap buhay 'Merica—Life is hard in America.

Glutathione

Erase the brown blemishes your
ancestors left behind

Iitim ka!–you'll get dark!
Your Tita yells at you.
But you blossom under a blanket of sunshine.
Rays kiss your skin, revealing the fingerprints of your
ancestors' love
leaving a familiar scent on your head, a departing gift.

This is the feeling of acceptance.

But your Tita yells,
Susunugin ka ng araw!–The sun will burn you!
Suddenly, you grow afraid of stepping into a pool of
warm embraces.
You sneer at the sun's departing gift and
hide away from its glowing rays.

When you learn to hate the sun and its love,
you learn to hate the skin the heavens painted you in.

So, you drench yourself in a sea of glutathione,
dip your elbows in white-out,
scrub the melanin off your skin,
ball your fists to form white knuckles,
hold your breath to turn pale,
until you've
muted the brave faces of your ancestors
with the fear of glowing like the sun and
being as rich as the Earth.

Paról

The fire of the Pilipino spirit lies deep in its indigo waters where
Window-Payne oysters peek out of waves, glimmering
underneath streams of sun,
coating translucent shells in glowing rainbows.
They catch the attention of a child who gives them to
her Father.
He molds them softly into the brightest stars she has
never seen,
the soft glow of stars in this city drowns in
thick clouds of dust and smog from sputtering *Jeepenys*
and *Tricycles*.

But this star emerges from the fog of city lights and noise,
Taken from the sea into gentle, loving hands,
this *paról* inspires wish-filled milky ways and galaxies of
hope
that trump the fading light of suffocating stars
in the Philippine Christmas wind.

Araw at Bituin
(Sun and Stars)

The glow of the Sun spills elegantly across cerulean waters,
it awakens in the cool dawn air,
stretches eight arms across the sky,
letting out a bellowing yawn which
gently nudges the islands from their nap as they
fill life into leafy Philippine jungles and
melodies of calm into foamy waves resting on the shore.

When dusk strokes its indigo paint across the sky, the Sun
sings lullabies to this war-torn island,
takes out three night light stars,
pins them in velvet clouds,
calls them Freedom, Justice, Peace.
The lights shine softly over Luzon, Visayas, and Mindanao;
buries their galaxy dust in soil
hoping it'll sprout stems of hope that can
embrace the land when it weeps.

Tumaba Ka (You Got Fat)

Every family party is an existential dread.
Every shift in weight transforms into a dramatic gasp of
a crowd of titas who have watched one too many
teleseryes–dramas,
thinly tattooed eyebrows float among a wide sea of
wrinkled foreheads
and suddenly, a flock of short, ebony curls come rushing
to you,
armed with the blades of unnecessary comments
and concerns,
cutting through the thickest of skin and the hardest
of hearts,
pinching aortic flabs until they rip and fall apart
like how we all wish our rolls fall apart when titas
pinch the skin hanging off our bones like limp *camisetas*
on clotheslines
or rub our bellies, wishing us good luck in finding a suitor
who would
dare take our *longanisa* fingers in their hand.

Titas trace their famished fingers on the backs of
our thighs,
counting cellulite like tally marks,
each faint line a point that goes towards this game of
fatphobia,
whoever wins
gets skinny,
gets suitors,
gets compliments,
gets married

gets to be the one who deflects stabs of guilt and
sentences that start with *when I was your age I was only X
lbs.* or
the piercing slash of side eyes and judgmental glares at the
dinner table,
eyeing every grain of rice on your plate,
and every chunk of meat on your fork,
as if you'll just stuff it all in your face

Fatphobia's buried so deep in our culture it
becomes a formal greeting.
Tumaba Ka replaces *Mabuhay* on welcome mats and
travel signs.
They invite you to family parties just to
slash you with their *chismis t*ongues and
cut your skin deeper than purple stretchmarks,

these scars don't fade away.

It ripples permanently in stagnant toilet water and
again in whirlpool flushes.
It's spelled out with untouched rice
scattered on squeaky plates or
burnt tastebuds from
acid waterfalls

And you attend these family parties anyway,
mostly because your mom tells you so.
But this time, you walk in like the
main character of a *teleserye,*
nose in the air as you pass your
kontrabida titas,

deflecting sharp tongues and piercing glares,
piling your plate with rice and another bowl of *ulam,*
stuff your face and chew loud because
you have the thickest of skin and the hardest of hearts

Clothespin

Take the clothespin and clip it on your nose
the pressure on your cartilage will force it to rise.
We don't want Chocolate Hills,
only Purple Mountain Majesties.[15]
Don't mind the Red from the pressure
or the Blue from the pain,
that's part of the transformation.
Just scrub yourself White and soon enough,
you'll blend in with all of our star-spangled glory.
Soon enough, you'll be
beautifully palatable for our colonized tongues.

Keep the clothespin and wear it to sleep.
Let the shape harden overnight and maybe,
they'll air you on TFC
Pinch the bridge for good luck and maybe,
they won't call you *pango–flat-nosed*
Squeeze your nostrils in, don't blow them out,
so you'll finally be *maganda–beautiful*

Hopefully, your DNA will do somersaults, and
launch itself to the Dreamland.
Twist and turn away from the Homeland, maybe you'll
get a white man to slip a ring on your finger and
generate generations of Chocolate Hills buried under
Purple Mountain Majesties
who won't have to landscape their terrain with clothespins

---

15   William Arms Fisher and Katherine Lee Bates, "America the Beautiful"
       (Oliver Ditson Company, 1917).

who won't have to flip-flop their DNA and launch
themselves to
an unfamiliar Dreamland
you won't have to worry whether your children are
palatable enough for colonized tongues.

But, I heard that when you pinch your nose and gulp air
three times
you can stop hiccups.
So while you wear your clothespin,
I hope you swallow enough wind to realize that the Stars
and the Sun are
blown away by Chocolate Hills more than
Purple Mountain Majesties.
While you wear your clothespin,
I hope you inhale tornadoes that can bend the metal and
snap the wood that suffocates your nose and
I hope you can launch yourself back to your Homeland and
realize that it has always been your Dreamland
And I hope that when you sit atop of those Chocolate Hills,
with the wind gusting in your hair,
this hiccup of colonized beauty stops punching your lungs
like they punched our ancestors.

And I hope you feel the warmth of the Stars and the Sun,
embrace the soil beneath your palms,
and listen to your Home, calling you
maganda.

Pinayism

Envy is a parasite planted by the patriarchy
intertwined in vines that grow
out of a Pinay's delicate fingers.

Promises of sisterhood and friendship
infected and burned by the stench of
a man's breath, commanding we fight
each other like lionesses, then serve them
a silver plate of voluptuous meat picked and
shaved off of our bare bones

Parasites push us to please the patriarchy,
love the patriarchy, feed the patriarchy
until we starve our sisters of promises of
love we once pinky-swore of giving.

Perhaps, we can start growing
instead of eye rolling and side-eyeing each other
to the death just for a place on a silver plate
these men sloppily eat off of.

I am not your enemy, I am your sister.
Let us not put down but grow with each other.
Let us intertwine our severed vines and begin to
climb out of the overgrown and unkempt woods of
the imaginary war between women that we have been
gaslit into believing.

Let us hold each other's delicate, war-torn fingers
stained with the remnants of this patriarchal parasite.
Mag sama sama tayong mga Pinay–let's unite as Pinays

Children of the Diaspora

Our culture smells of *sukà* and *toyo–vinegar* and *soy sauce*
and the steam of fresh Jasmine rice.
It's drunken Karaoke nights,
having two first names and
the fish aisle of *Seafood City.*
It's *if you're Asian, how come you have a Latino last name?*

It's confusion and chaos,
frustration and fraught,
shame and trying to be
everything that you're not.
It's *I'm mixed Spanish and Chinese*

It's stretching your muscles to its thinnest threads
just to dip your fingers in salty, crystal waters and
prop your elbows up against hot volcanoes,
taking in the beauty of a country that
never felt like yours.
But the kisses of warm rain,
and soft hugs from volcanic soil
invite you to stay anyway.

It's admiring islands from thousands of miles away
and feeling stuck in a place you never chose to stay
it's untangling twisted tongues and
the aching regret of not understanding Pilipino dramas or
the stories of your *lolos* and *lolas.*

It is language and literature,
history and rediscovery,
it's finding yourself and
fighting for the fruit of culture
ripped away from your stems
the minute you sprouted in
a land with cold rain and hard soil.

"Sorry"

Is what I say to the corner of the kitchen table before
I say "ow!" or *"aray!"*
Acknowledging its hurt before mine,
fully knowing that it's inanimate,
barren of sensory neurons and emotions,
but I still apologize
even though it has bruised my hips purple,
punctured my bones and scraped my skin because
I was taught to have good manners.

Mag sorry ka, mag thank you ka–Say please and thank you,
to always take the blame because
it's better to be the bigger, more mature person even if this
world forces you to shrivel into a scrap-paper ball.

But don't act *too mature,* he might think you're older than
you seem.

You're misleading them. Act your age.
You're not saying "po" after each sentence
so he probably thinks you're older,
show some respect.

But they're 50 years-old and I'm just in 6th grade—–

Huag ka sumagot saakin–don't talk back to me.

Sorry, po

So I continue to shrink my insides, hoping I
grow small enough to go unnoticed—

Maybe this time, I can wear my favorite dress on the
Metro Red Line
and scurry away before the old guy on the 7:30am
Westbound notices.

Maybe this time, the creepy relative won't ask a ten year
old for hugs and kisses

But this time,
I crumple myself up so small, I can feel the layers of
unsolicited apologies press against my pinched cheeks
and bruised hips.

The echoes of
*sorry*s and *my bads*
fill tunnels in my head
until my ears explode into strings of
internalized misogyny

and I realize that all this time,
I've been apologizing for scars
that were never my fault

So I unravel my crumpled,
scrap-paper heart,
straighten it out and
erase the words

sorry po

Nipis
(Thin/Sensitive)

Empathy is often confused for sensitivity.

Too emotional, too weak,
too over dramatic,
it's only attention you seek—

So we're forced to grow thick layers of skin,
tough enough to deflect sharp shards of insults,
dark thoughts, sad feelings.

But I guess I was born with onion skin,
brittle, crumbly,
easily pulverized by snarky words and
slight changes in mood.
Tears fall like loose snow,
and when lightning strikes, my chest
heaves and explodes into an avalanche
unstoppable waves of ice
rolling

tumbling
crashing

down.

Tears swirl into hurricanes that
slurp up my heart in a tornado,
my chest pulses and bursts into firecracker sobs
but then they'd tell me
masyadong kang manipis–you are too sensitive

So I swallow down the hurricanes
blow out my tornadoes and
patch up the holes in my onion skin,
hold my head above water and keep
gasping for air

Stockholm Syndrome

The crashing rivers of colonialism
erode so deep into our minds, we
pray for our children to wear the white skin
of our colonizers.

We beg for Spaniard blood to shine through and
fight off the melanin gifted to us by the
the Philippine sun and soil.

They say to eat the seeds of white fruit,
wash the rice twice and drink its
pristine milky color.
Gulp it down for your fetus and
sing songs in Spanish––make sure to include the lisp,
it's the only way a child can wear the skin of your great-
grandmother's captors,
the ones who held her by the wrists and spoon-fed her
heapings of trauma that she
brings as *pasalubong–souvenirs* to the family party.

She wraps her trauma in pretty pieces of
Stockholm Syndrome.
We open them,
and like Pandora, release trauma's daughters called
colorism and colonial mentality who teach us to
fall in love with our oppressors, from their
pale, blood-stained skin to the shards on their bones

so when we look at the mirror
that glows with the reflection of our ancestors,
we only see imposters,
 wearing skin they're not supposed to own

Bayanihan

There's still identity in this country named after a stranger
from a foreign land,
still beauty in this culture that's been molded to the shape
of guns and bombs by people who
grip these islands in a chokehold.

No, this beauty does not lie in the cerulean waters
of Palawan,
the smooth grace of whale sharks in Cebu or
any of the white-sand beaches plastered on airport walls and
the videos of white tourists searching for wanderlust
and awe.

It lies in the bony man wearing a *sando–tank* top and
tsienalas–slippers,
carrying the weight of 20 children in two pots that swing
on a stick as skinny as his arms,
yelling *Taho! Taho!* to the children running in school
uniforms and black shoes.
And after a day of filling small stomachs with sweet syrup
and soft tofu,
he sings happily home with empty pots and a pocket full of
change enough to last the next day.

It lies in the *lola–grandmother* and her *apo–grandchild* by
the *simbahan–church,*
slipping soft buds of *Sampaguitas* in garlands, and
wrapping it around the necks of Saints and Mama Mary
to offer prayers for the sick and the poor
before they walk home to their *kubo–hut.*

It lies in the people
barefoot and brown
skin swimming in wet air and golden sun,
singing on rooftops floating in floods,
knee deep in murky waters,
smiles stretched across their faces
holding the hands of their *kababayans–fellow countrymen*
carrying huts on their backs in search of a new home

CHAPTER 3

REVOLUTION AND REVELATION

Rebelling against reigns of terror who want nothing but to
Eat your spirits alive begins with raising your
Voices louder than the rolling sound of thunder,
   avalanches or
Oceans drowning, gurgling in their own blackholes. It
   starts with
Learning how to extinguish your own wildfires lit by
   arsonists who have
Usurped power from lightning to fuel embers of hate.
Take the ashes of your blown-out flames, turn it into soil,
Ingrain seeds into your heart, let them bloom into roses
   shaped like closed fists, raise them in the air.
Open the petals and out comes a bare palm, feeling the
   warmth of the sun. Revolutions begin when we
Notice the way rain falls wistfully on petals emerging in the
   morning dew after a typhoon

Raised fists eventually turn into open palms that hold the
Earth so tenderly they foster a garden tilled with
Volition and unity. A land more peaceful than
Eden's. One that grows trees free of judgement and fruit free
    of guilt. This is a
Land of Love. Yes, one that truly believes in *all* forms of
    love. I still
Aspire to one day open my raised fist and reveal a soft palm,
Turn all the fallen ashes from wildfires and volcanoes
Into diamond seeds that do not sprout of greed but
    shimmer light
Onto shadows of fear who deprive tender buds from the
    peaceful sun. I will
Never let myself soak under reigns of terror, I will, instead,
    control the thunder.

Dirty Words

Since when did *actibista*[16] become a dirty word?
Since when did *rebelde*[17] become a taboo term?
Did it start the day the sculptor finished smoothing out the
edges of Marcos' stone-cold skin?
Or was it the day they dumped our history books in
puddles of white-out?

We drive by the *Katipunan* monument[18] and cheer for our
victory
against those who imprisoned our ancestors and the
bravery of those who believed strongly enough in the
freedom of our people.
But as soon as we pass *EDSA*,[19] we forget how dirty words and
taboo terms shaped the very soil we sink our toes in

Why is a revolution only acceptable when it is a part of our
history
and disrespectful when it is in our present?

---

16   Activist.
17   Rebel.
18   Also known as the Bonifacio Monument that commemorates Philippine
     hero Andrés Bonifacio's fight against Spanish colonial rule.
19   Epifanio de los Santos Avenue, a highway around Manila, Philippines.

Oust

Oppressing the poor and hungry, he rides on the
Underbelly of a fascist dragon,
Shooting the innocent, the activists
Tromping on the Indigenous and the children

Digging himself deeper in a quicksand of lies, he
Undoes the work of our revolutionary history. But,
There is hope in the youth who dream.
Emerging from the streets to march and
Riot for a future molded by the hands of the people.
They sing for justice, raise their fists in the air,
Erupting with resilience and fearlessness to overthrow, if
they so dare.

Acrostic

Fascism is *not* the word they use in
United States History classes to describe the
Classist, cocky, cowards of the
KKK

Don't even try to say the word:
Oligarchs, when referring to Congress, who sell their souls
to the
NRA, who stuff bullets and bills in their suit pockets,
trading their empathy for
Apathy and apparently argue the whole day away until
there are clear winners and
Losers in the most expensive playground in America,
located in the great
District of Columbia—a house dedicated to the grim face
of Indigenous genocide and

Taking away children from families and making dreamers
and seekers
Run faster than the rain of bullets chasing them in midair.
United is far from the State of our nation. One filled with
Money mongrels and maniacs who don't care about
People—just power and pennies in their pockets

Bad Apples

Axing down a system that wrongfully
Criminalizes Black and Brown bodies is not
A radical idea once you realize that the roots of the tree
have been
Bastardized and poisoned since its inception.

All of its fruits are contaminated, even the ones that look
Clean and crisp to the bite. Those still grow next to
Abhorrent apples, polluted with the stench of Jim Crow's
breath. They
Brutalize the intestines of their victims who dare sink their
teeth in them

And of course, you may say this is all false because *you*
have picked a fruit that tastes like
Candy in your mouth, whose juices stain beautifully on
your porcelain skin. But,
Allowing others to die at the hands of your predestined
luck is like
Blaming your friend's death on their wrongful choice of
picking a poisoned fruit on an

Already poisoned tree that you just so happened to benefit
from *once* even though
Countless victims have fallen under its war-torn wrath
and racist rage, the tree will always
Acquit its fruit, fully knowing the depth of its guilty toxins.
So don't be surprised when
Bad apples continue to grow on perfectly poisoned trees
that you refuse to axe down.

Dare to Struggle, Do not be Afraid

Dare to remove the brick that collapses an entire empire.
To change a country, we must rebuild cities from scratch. Though we may
struggle to carry the rubble in our arms and the concrete on our feet, please
do this so light can finally pierce through corrupt cities and politicians.
Do not do this for yourselves, but for those who have only dreamed of light.
Be the person who liberates the *masa*. Be the person who ensures no one is
afraid of puppets connected to sticky fingers that smell of dirty money.

Peaceful Protest

Outraged when people take to the streets
to shout for the voices of the unheard, the
unserved, the ones who lay cold on the floor when
uninvited bullets burst through their front door.

A protest is peaceful until it's disturbed by
the loud clack of batons,
the pounding of bullets,
the hiss of tear gas ready to sink its fangs deep
in innocent eye sockets.

Listen to the cries of mothers who lost their sons and
daughters to the unjust and unfair.
Protesting about damaged property over people
does not mean you care

when a white man sprays bullets in a church
in a concert or a crowd and
splatters red on white walls that would
make Jackson Pollock proud,
not a single breath of concern comes out of
anybody's mouth.

That's just the way things are—

is no longer an excuse
for shooting, murdering
and letting cops on the loose

A protest is peaceful until it is disturbed.
Remember,
riots are the language of the unheard[20]

---

20 Dr. Martin Luther King, "The Other America" (speech, Stanford, CA, presented April 4, 1967).

Hands Behind Your Back

The cop says: *put your hands behind your back like
you're praying,*

but he's already recited the rosary 20 times since catching
flashes of red, white and blue, on his skin.
He freezes. He shakes:
I'm nervous, sir.

Do you have reason to be?

He learns that every moment he willingly stood under
the night sky on the 4th of July could not prepare him
for the sound of explosions or the flash of patriotic lights
or the way white people tromp around the grass,
looking for a spot to take,
a body to break

Do you have a weapon? Kneel!

No church prayer and worship
could prepare his knees for the cold, hard pavement
crushing his bones
and every conversation with God could not train him
for the moment his fate fell on someone else's hands.

Get down, search him.

They flatten him like they're tracing an outline of a body in
a crime scene
He's now prayed the rosary more times than cop cars have

flashed life before his ancestors' eyes
But he holds his hands together like he's praying,
rosary wrapped around his neck, cop fingers still
dipped inside pools of panicky breath

You're free.

And flashes of red, white, and blue speed away.
His life back in God's fate
but he still keeps his hands together, somehow still bound
to the ghost of Jim Crow

unable to liberate.

To Zara: Together We Rise, Kasama[21]

Together we rise, Kasama
with the people and with the masses,
because one voice is enough noise
to get the attention of two—
which turns into a hundred
until we have composed a musical masterpiece called
the song of freedom
that rings in each thump of a Kasama's heart
and bellows in the throats of every chant of change.
It's the rhythm under the stomp of our feet as we
march on the concrete,
it's the food that satiates our hunger on strike,
reminding us that there is no better nourishment than
the emancipation of our people.

Together we rise, Kasama
Resist the screeches of fear and terror
that interrupt our revolutionary choir.
You conduct, and we sing louder,
harmonizing our liberation to the perfect key.
Resist those who scream we fall flat or pitchy—
We know our voices have the power to
fuel beats and rhythms to last for generations,
the louder we are, the more people will belt out our song
until we have muted the shrieks of fascism

---

21   Companion.

You have the strength, Kasama
escaped for us, Kasama
your spirit and soul still thrive in us, Kasama.

We will continue your revolutionary song,
Even when you are gone.

To the Lumad: There Is Power In The Youth Who Dream

There is power in the youth who dream
Those who have witnessed their fallen atés [22]and kuyas[23],
Those who have buried their nanays[24] and tatays[25],
Those who fearlessly stand in front of creaky chalkboards,
scraping letters and numbers with charcoal,
scribbling on banana leaves with broken pencils,
planting revolution and courage into the hearts of the young
that bloom into melodies and harmonies.
Water their leaves with the strength and power to
deflect bullets raining from the sky,
Do not run from the calm of the Mindanao fields,
let your songs of freedom grow louder,
let your story ring in their ears,
There is power in the youth who sing

They cannot know truth
They cannot know revolution
They cannot know dreams
They cannot know education
Starve them. Bomb them. Kill them.
There is danger in the youth who dream

---

22 Older Sisters.
23 Older Brothers.
24 Mothers.
25 Fathers.

Let your roots expand on your rightful land,
knot the ends to edges of Earth your lolos[26] and lolas[27] tilled.
Arm yourselves with a pencil and a song
And when you are met with knives and tanks,
know that you will always have the upper-hand.
They shake, quiver, and
call the children *communists* just to feel better.

Sing your song and sing it loud
Make their ears ring,
harper a bellow in front of a crowd
Your revolutionary fervor will echo through your
rightful land,
vibrate through the roots knotted at the Earth's ends.
Your lolos, lolas, nanays, tatays, atés, and kuyas survive in
your heart,
hear their voices and summon their strength when you're
falling apart.
The blueprint of the future lies in a banana leaf scroll
tucked in your back pocket.
Let your tongue sing of your people.
Engrave your history in charcoal on the trees and skies,
Remember your rights:

You are truth
You are revolution
You are your ancestor's biggest dreams
You are education

---

26   Grandmothers.
27   Grandfathers.

Resist. Rebel. Refuse.

Raise your fists and and let your voices sting
There is power in the youth who sing

Close your eyes, your future is more peaceful than
what it seems
There is power in the youth who dream

The X in Pilipinx

If our language is so gender neutral,
then why does homophobia still plague our land?
Why does transphobia's poison still seep into our
white sands?

Drag is okay, as long as it's just a TV show
Call it tomboy,
not lesbian,
it has a better undertone

Our language's pronouns may not see gender,
but our culture still uses it as a weapon.
The X in Pilipinx is a seed that will one day
uproot the trunk of *machismo* in our language.

The X in Pilipinx rips out the petals of sexism,
so blatant in our culture it is normalized in speech.
Our language cannot be neutral when the god of patriarchy
sits comfortably in his seat.

The X in Pilipinx raises its fists to the soldiers
of colonization,
welcomes the non-binary with open hands and
sifts out hate from our white sands

The Audacity Award Goes To: Men

We've set the bar so low for men
that when they
touch this bar
ever
so
slightly
with the curve of their
dirty,
unclipped
fingernails,
they want a trophy wife
shaped with the golden curves
of a woman's sacred body,
where they can wrap their

unwashed,
sour hands
on our hips,
dig into our skin with their fingertips

then they start their acceptance speeches
and bring up all the five times
they did the bare minimum like
when they helped their mom
get the groceries or
be nice and polite
then suddenly, they expect
a certificate of participation
a coupon for free entry
a buy 1 get 1 meal

and the world gives it to them
with a standing ovation and a round of applause
their mothers pinch their slimy cheeks
their fathers give them a gross wink
tell them *"ATTA BOY!"*
then they walk off the stage
underdressed, with too much Axe spray,
nail-biter fingernails and a hole in their shoes,
the magazines call them humble and down-to-Earth

LOOK! Here's a man going grocery shopping!
OVER THERE! A man being present for his children!
DID YOU KNOW? He accompanied me to my
doctor appointments?
WOW! Get the cameras! Put this in the history books!
A man went slightly above the bar!
Get him his coupon, he deserves a free meal
get him a third trophy wife for being a decent fucking
human being

Then he'll smack the crevices of that voluptuous trophy
with his greasy lips and the audience will cheer
and the cycle will go on over
and over
again because

we have been taught to purse our lips,
delete the threads and block the accounts,

Stay silent,

Don't cause a scene, people will stare.
If we cry wolf we'll be called

heartless,
stone cold
bitches
and liars
who won't *give nice boys a chance*
and whores who *post pictures asking for it*
but *wasn't he nice?* they ask.

Questions like this are why mama's boys cry *"nice boys
finish last"*
and why women hear that phrase and feel bad
as if the history books don't show that men have *never*
come in last

Questions like this are why magazines still call women
whores,
and sluts,
and bitches without a heart

this is why crowds don't cheer for women who are
underdressed
or for women who are overdressed

or why crickets fill the room when we get
groceries or accompany our husbands to get the flu shot
*because they still don't know how to fill out the fucking
paperwork*

this is all because they keep
setting and
resetting our bar
until we don't know

what the fuck or
where the fuck
this fucking bar is anymore

I'm a tired, angry woman who keeps witnessing men
win trophy wife awards that they smother in their
dirty,
lonely,
sticky hands
that they think they have
earned,
deserved or
are entitled to
because of the five whole times they were a considerate
human being
in this patriarchal piazza
and we're supposed to stay silent with pursed lips and
nervous thumbs
not holding a single medal
because all of our bodies and souls have been awarded as
perfect attendance awards
to subpar men who want to feel better about themselves

so men,
here's another award
an award that you *truly* deserve
that you have *truly* earned

and it's for having

the fucking

audacity.

I Don't Speak to Homophobes

I don't speak to homophobes,
especially the ones who go to church and sing:
Love thy neighbor
that is until they find out
their neighbor loves the wrong gender.

I don't speak to homophobes,
Particularly the ones who proudly say
Adam and Eve, not Adam and Steve
like it's a Pulitzer Prize-Winning, debate-wrecking
argument, beautiful enough to be engraved on
the arches of anti-gay rhetoric.

I don't speak to homophobes,
specifically the ones who take pictures of
rainbow-painted skies, posted with the caption
Live Laugh Love
and then proceed to burn down rainbow flags with
flames of hate and hypocrisy,
take the ashes and sprinkle it on the faces of
people who have finally mustered the courage to
unlock the closet and soak in the sun, only to be met with
the remnants of their Pride.

I don't speak to homophobes
because I simply can't imagine how
anyone could be so bothered by love
or take time the time to beg their creator to rip rainbows
from the sky until the stars bleed Rancor Red and Binary Blue

Flight Haiku

I will endeavor
through harsh winds and flaming stars
my flight is endless

Dear Mother of Exiles[28]

Dear Mother of Exiles,

You were a mighty woman, said to have imprisoned
Zeus' bolt
Not guarding, but lighting the way for the tired and
the poor
the huddled masses, the homeless, and the exiles across
many shores

But now, you weep
and your flame, extinguished
Your face marked with streaks
for the ones nearly diminished

You were made to symbolize world-wide welcome
with mild, calm, and proud eyes
eager to guide and embrace the dreamers of Ellis Island
who no longer have to run or hide

But now you are an empty metaphor
filled with abandoned nests,
crusted with pollution and greed

---

28 Emma Lazarus, "The New Colossus" (New York: Inscription carving, 1883).

A little girl once asked me why you wore a jail cell atop
your head
Your crown, once a symbol of strength
now looks like barbed wire
trapping the dreamers, refugees, and exiles
you swore to protect and guide with your fire

What do you do when the tired and the poor
are tempest-tost within their own shores?

The Statue of Liberty in Shackles

Broken shackles
replaced with the book of liberation
"You've always been free"

"Hold on to this fire"
"Don't tell them we're using it to burn their
dignity"

Shackles taken from her hand
strapped to her ankles
"Now stay there and look pretty for
postcards and pictures"

The drapes hide scars and craters so deep
they carry the echoes of a
lashing whip
and the sizzle of a
branding iron

They tuck in the
ball and chain under her dress
kissed it goodnight and sang
"Sleep tight, history will be erased tonight"

Erase the face of Black Liberty
outline it with the blueprint of Manifest Destiny
carve her eyes and fill them with genocidal fervor
gleaming from sea to shining sea, she looks at her

reflection
and sees
the face of Columbia

Shred the pages of history books
Edit.

Delete.

Backspace.

Call it indentured servitude
"Remember, a Republican freed them all"

"This is freedom," tourists whisper on a ferry
They stare in awe at her crown,
her gleaming eyes, the fire and the book of justice

But they cannot see the chains hidden underneath
They cannot see the lashes and craters
They cannot hear the wind of the whip, the sizzle of the
branding iron
or the cries for help
They cannot see the shadows of a Black woman erased
banging against copper walls, screaming to be saved

How can we call this country the land of the free
when our symbol of liberation is enslaved?

On Monuments

We cannot rely on monuments to remember our history.
Though they may outlast the artist who molded them,
they don't last in the memories of those who glance out of
their car windows then swiftly drive away or those who
stop to admire their height and detail then
skim through the tablet of text that holds the
stories of a frozen moment.

If massive blocks of art held hostage in time
still cannot remind us of what we celebrated in the past,
or what we should do in the future,
and we continue to skim the surface instead of
reaching into the core of every
marble mold and metal sculpture, then
monuments are nothing but
the Earth's paperweights, filled with the
ashes of important memories and
world-shaking events that we will
never care to investigate.

Slander

If I can't say it,
then they shouldn't either.
If they think it's so wrong,
why do they keep using it
in all of their songs?

But even if slander is extracted and erased
from the vocabulary of an entire ethnicity or race
whose necks are still held by the rope
of words meant to strangle and strip them of hope,
the Earth's waters hold memories 400 years old
that soak into the skin of those whose hearts are too cold,
and mouths too stiff,
forced to believe that slavery's a myth.
Dew drops melt and nourish seeds of hate in their
poisoned hearts
and these words of slander are never taken apart.

Performative

You don't have to wear someone's skin
or button yourself up in their melanin
to know the pain of seven bullets in the back.

You don't have to put yourself in
a voluntary chokehold to know the
pain of veins popping,
or the slash of air
piercing windpipes open.

Empathy is helpful, but we only need Humanity
to understand why we must
Amplify
Fight
Uplift and
Expand our activism outside of our
selected experiences

Black Liberation, Indigenous Liberation
is
Liberation
for all

Golden Shovel: Bayan Ko? (My Country?)

Ang bayan ko ng Pilipinas–My country, the Philippines:
Lupa ng ginto at bulaklak–Land of gold, garden of flowers
Pagibig ang sa kanyang palad–Endowed with love,
Nag-alay ng ganda at dilag–Gifted with beauty and radiance,

At sa kanyang yumi at ganda–Intoxicated because of her beauty,
dayuhan ay nahalina–Foreign lands were drawn to her.
Bayan ko–My dear country,
binihag ka–They came and conquered you
nasadlak sa dusa–And you suffered in misery.

-BAYAN KO, JOSÉ CORAZON DE JESUS, TRANSLATION
BY PHILIPPINE STUDY GROUP OF MINNESOTA[29]

I must find **my**
way around this **country**
I'm forced to call home. They say I must replace **the**
sweet, humid memories of the **Philippines**
with dreams of this supposed ***Land***
of the free and *home* **of**
the slaves whose masters stuff **gold**
in their pockets, bury skeletons in their **garden**
and dance on their graves. This is far from the land **of**
promises where they say opportunity **flowers**
in every bush and stem. This land **endowed**
with people who hold its soil **with**
careful hands, who water seeds with tears of **love**

---

29   Jose Corazon de Jesus, "Bayan Ko." Translated by Philippine Study Group of Minnesota. *Crossroads Resource Center,* accessed June 12, 2020.

all terrorized by the same men an ocean away
who think they **gifted**
this archipelago with blessings of terror.
Men who came **with**
gunpowder and left behind ashes. Men who have
tainted the **beauty**
of these islands I can no longer call home.
The people trapped in this land of the free **and**
home of the brave are restless and afraid.
This country has dulled my skin of the **radiance**
from the Philippine sun and has **intoxicated**
the flicker of three lonely stars in my heart. But **because**
we've painted this cage with bright stars and
bold stripes, all **of**
the free birds willingly flutter to their captors,
away from the Motherland. Leaving **Her**
wondering if Her sampaguitas hold the same **beauty**
as bloody roses. Perhaps it is because our culture
holds what is most **foreign**
as more beautiful, and after a while, these
familiar tropical **lands**
become an eyesore, even though they **were**
once an unconquered paradise white men were **drawn**
to invade, ingesting every tropical fruit and
indigenous body **to**
their bare bones. My Motherland wonders why **Her**
children with broad, beautiful wings would willingly
get them clipped. **My**
Motherland whistles the songs of freedom but her **dear**
birds have found comfort in peeking through iron
bars in their new **country.**

I must find my way around this cage with
clipped wings. **They**
tell me I should be grateful for the first birds
who willingly **came**
into this rusty cage, once speckled in stars **and**
stripes, but it is hard to survive in a country that **conquered**
your Motherland and pulverized your ancestors
into gunpowder. **You**
begin to believe that living and surviving are synonyms **and**
become accustomed to peering out of iron bars
and believing that **you**
live in the greatest country in the world because
other lands have **suffered**
under its imperial power and violence. But I will
flap my wings **in**
this cage of a foreign land I'm forced to call home
and put out the flames of my ancestors' **misery**.

CHAPTER 4

IDENTITY

———

Islands I remember and recognize, yet cannot claim
dance elegantly 11,756 km away. I
envy the way the sea recognizes Its lush, emerald mane,
   how the sun
nestles softly under the nape of Its neck, napping. I'm
   jealous of
the way It's familiar with everyone, knowing every
   pangalan–name but mine.
I can't blame It; the mirror can't even remember a
time where I made eye-contact. Perhaps it's because I refuse
   to see myself
yearning or mourning for a Motherland who spit me out
   and will not let me back in.

Mutt

The middle school boy says:

Chinese? Japanese?
Last name sounds Hispanic,
are you Mexican? Spanish?

Are you from the islands?
Like the people who live in huts?
Or are you all of the above,
like some kind of mutt?

He smiles, then barks.

Goosebumps crawl up my neck like angry red ants,
fists clamped so tight my knuckles form snowcaps.
If one more micro-aggression lands on the pile of insults
on my shoulders,
an avalanche will come crashing down my chest.
My heart will sink into freezing cold waters and
overflow into lakes in my eyes

He barks again. You're an inbred.

My feet are glued on to glaciers,
tongue still caught in frost bite,
and voice still lost in Arctic fog.

I cannot surrender to the cold, so I
release my fists and melt my snowcapped knuckles.
I pat down the snow piled onto my chest like wet sand,

play lifeguard and carry my heart out the water,
desperately blowing back life into its
withered walls and torn heartstrings,

Bark at me, mutt.

I have always let my rage turn into tears,
then loneliness, and finally

silence.

The boy walks away and laughs, still barking.
My voice, still lost,
lips still frozen.
So instead of barking or biting,
I try to repaint the warm landscape of home
in this deserted iceberg land.

Blank,
White,
Cold.

I try to conjure watercolor memories of tropical islands,
but even those were lost somewhere in the
snowstorm or tossed into mounds of hail.

So I wait for the day the snow melts into the Philippine sea,
and when this day comes, perhaps my masterpiece
won't have to be painted in shades of distant memories.

Ambiguous Portrait

I am a blank canvas ready to be splattered with
incoherent guesses of countryside landscapes I *sort of*
look like.

Although, I could've sworn I was once an oil painting filled
with the
glow of rice paddy sunsets, wispy brushes of
bahay kubos–cubed houses,
and farmers crouched over,
knee-deep into waters with
caribous in the back.

I guess my scenery was *too ambiguou*s
to be hung prettily on a blank wall.
Someone must have bought gallons of bleach to
white out my culture from an art gallery or perhaps
out of this body who can't even remember its own lineage,
whose voice still ping-pongs in stutters when mistaken for
another painting.

Pilipinos to an American

Look at how desperate they are to reach for a
culture they know nothing about.
Baybayin[30] character tattoos inscribed on their backs as
they
turn away from a country they so badly want to call
theirs.

The *characters* cry for help; they're getting kidnapped.
Taken to a country surrounded by people who know
nothing about
the ink squeezed from the ashes of *Pinatubo,*
who fantasize about ancestors and villages they see in
the movies.
Look at how their hands uncomfortably pinch the rice,
their fingertips
scrape the banana leaves as if they're digging for
fine China.

That is not how you *act* Pilipino.

I should know, I am the motherland.
Stop using Pilipinx. We don't see gender.
Do not butt into our politics, you do not get to talk
while you're tucked away in air-conditioned rooms and
newly paved roads.

---

30   Pre-Hispanic Philippine script/writing system

You're so whitewashed.
Baybayin characters may glimmer on your skin under the
rays of the Philippine sun,
Your voice may sound like the crash of waves hitting
Palawan sands
Your heart may be shaped like a Manila Mango but
we are not alike.

You do not know struggle,
You cannot know grief
You do not know me.

Eldest Daughter Syndrome

They say 99 percent of Eldest Daughters suffer from back pain

it may be caused by carrying textbooks filled with a
colonized past
and forcibly ingesting every American fact and
the accomplishments of dead white men
just to pass a class.

It may also be from holding on to
one too many photo albums and
hoarding daydreams of the Motherland,
reminiscing the bellow of the caribou and the
crow of the rooster in the middle of the night,
because the Motherland is always awake and alive
ready to seize the day,
making sure Her people thrive.

The sun sinks into rice paddies like egg yolk bursting
on rice,
these images so faint and subtle, yet somehow more real than
being *here,*
in this land of survival and defeat
where Charging Bulls compete and eat the meat of
immigrant daughters, so naive and yet so grown
expected to succeed in a land that is not their home
bending over backwards to hop-scotch on
slippery milestones their parents left behind

They say back pain is also caused by
hunching over makeshift study tables
like second-hand kitchen counters or small business desks or
is it from tirelessly teaching siblings how to ace their next
test or
crouching over hour-long bubble baths and
scrambling to get the little ones dressed?

Eldest Daughters age twice as fast,
minds built for survival with steel hearts made to outlast
the bullies who pull on their twisted tongues
or teachers who tear through thick accents,
telling them *Tagalog* taints their top-notch training
of the *official* language of their newfound home.

But my diagnosis tells me 50 percent of my back pain is
from
carrying the weight of my parents' hopes,
and the beautiful burden of my ancestors' dreams.

Both are engraved in music notes in all three ossicles,
and swims between the Tres Marias where I
brush my index against its sparkling blue velvet sky,
hoping to connect-the-dots of my family's history to my
present
and perhaps erase my despair

Instead the stars tell me that the
other 50 percent of my back pain comes from
me.

The weights I strap on my ankles—the urgency to succeed.
The wave of electricity coursing through each nerve,
lighting fire in the marrow of my bones and
the palpitating urgency to run back to the
only home I've ever known.

Kamay (Hands)

My hands aren't elegant or long like mother's or father's
they're calloused and rough from
taking my anger out on pens,
pressing too hard on dull pencils,
and writing poetry on napkins no one will ever see

They're wrinkled and dry from
washing rice and dishes
and scrubbing mysterious liquids from the corners of
Mother's patient's house.
I still smell Lysol and Clorox sweating from my palms,
mothballs on my fingertips,
and the bitter smell of crushed painkillers underneath my
nail beds

They're short, stubby
and stuffed with the disappointment I felt when
the mood ring I stole from a gift shop got stuck half-way
through my pointer
and the shame rising to my cheeks when the security
guard told Mother,
the pain I felt from the *palò–hitting* I got on my hands
right after

They're heavy from years of being my Father's massage
therapist
after yet another overtime shift
I was convinced I had magnets for knuckles, drawn to the
knots on Father's tender muscles

Soil snuggles under my nails
from digging earthworms and fossils
when I was banished to the mud during recess
because the 3rd grade girls on the fresh grass said
I wasn't Asian enough to sit with them
because the 5th grade girls called me *Jungle Asian*

These hands hold food at the dinner table
sitting on warm banana leaves;
"Pinch the ulam[31] *and the rice with only one hand, then
push it into your mouth with your thumb,"* Mother smiles.
She packs me *adobo* for tomorrow's lunch.
I open my recycled yogurt container, ready to pinch my
rice but
kids pinch their noses and point at my short, stubby,
wrinkled, calloused, hands

*Do you eat with your hands because Filipinos are too poor
to use spoons and forks?*
they laugh, mouths wide,
rimmed with the bright orange grease of cafeteria pizza

My teacher asks me if my parents ever taught me how to
use utensils
"Yes it just tastes better this way"
*"But it's not the civilized way to eat, have you at least tried
chopsticks?"* she says, grabbing a fistful of fries.

---

31   Main Dish.

Ashamed, I took home plastic sporks and
found myself asking for permission to practice a tradition
I love
in my own home.

My Mother says: *"Did you already forget what I taught you?*
Pinch the ulam
and the rice, then
push it into your mouth with your thumb"

"Hindi ko nakalimutan, po" I replied
"I did not forget"

"Eh di gamitin mo yung kamay mo" she said.
"Then use your hands"

Kamayan is an ancestral revolutionary practice
that uses fingertips to untie the knots of colonization in
the cultural thread of eating
Even when these hands are beaten from
being thrown in the mud where *Jungle Asians* are
banished to,
Even when these thumbs are calloused from pushing
myself out of cultural holes where
people who are *not Asian enough* are trapped in,
I will hold onto my culture over warm banana leaves,
cushion it in a bed of rice and a blanket of *adobo*

And when these hands become cold and numb
I will warm my joints with the heat of my pen gliding
on paper,
igniting metaphors into fireworks and sparking similes
into bonfires
And I will pinch my stanzas, push them out with my
thumb
and unapologetically serve it on everybody's poetic plates
to consume

While elegantly, and boldly stating

Hindi ko makakalimutan–
I will not forget

5'3"

I am 5'3"
towering over Pilipino boys like the *Burj Khalifa*
Making me an undesirable selection to preserve their pride

I am 5'3"
too big, too bulky.
My family says, "When I was your age, I was petite!
Light enough so that men could swallow me whole.
So I can be safe in the pits of their inflated bellies
that matched their inflated pride.
I was small enough to be wanted,
to be an appetizer for their patriarchal hunger."

"While you," they mock, "you are too big to fit into
  their mouths.
You rip through their arrogant intestines.
You are not weak enough. You *must* be weak enough."

But I am 5'3" and I know two things
  1. Yes, my body is too big for my dwarfed confidence but
  2. The tallest building in the world is not the *Burj Khalifa*,
     2,722 feet tall.

It is me.
5'3" and unable to be swallowed whole.

Self-Forgiveness

Sometimes I think I have forgiven myself.
That I somehow convinced my brain that my mistakes cannot be fixed with
a fist to the heart, bruising my flesh and painting my skin so purple that
it erases my history of broken promises and bad decisions,
but it tricks me every time.

Every day, I wish I was a better friend, daughter, sister, granddaughter or just a
better person who can at least sprout or maybe even flower into someone worth trusting, caring for, or talking to.
Alas, I still plant seeds of doubt and they erupt into weeds of crippling self-hate

But, there are days where I finally tend to my garden and pull all the weeds out.
And there are days where I plant seeds that have bloomed into
self-love, acceptance, and peace
and even though there are times where my weeds crawl faster than my flowers bloom,
I remind myself of all the people I forgave
including *you*
and the people who came after and before *you*

When I remember how easy it is to forgive others,
I remember how even easier it should be to forgive myself.

So, Dear Self: Please accept when I have apologized.

Yellow

7: smiley faces and the
glimmering star stickers I'd proudly bring home from
school
It meant the waxy half-circle in the corner of my
masterpieces composed of
stick figures, my dream house, and butterflies
It meant Tatay's smile every time I'd mail it to him

11: the color of snow after taking the dog to Big Bear
and the light in Tatay's eyes after holding snow for the first
time
It was morning rays and melting butter tucked in between
Pan de Sal
But it also meant the slime Tatay coughed up sometimes
I don't really know what it was
I was too busy eating Pan de Sal

15: shame.
and hiding my skin
as everyone looked at me through sunflower-tinted lenses
slanting their eyes back and babbling "ching, chong, chang"
Calling me "Asian" as an insult, except it was just my
identity

17: It's the color of Tatay's skin, crumbling

17: the stains on Tatay's shirt and the walls of a cold empty
house

17: the color of accidents on white hospital sheets and IV
bags strapped to his arms

17: the snot running down my nose, yearning to have at
least called him one last time

17: It meant the sun flooding down the Philippine Sea, and
being afraid of the ocean but wishing to learn how to swim
across it
with a weight called "guilt" strapped to my heart,
just to see you one last time

17: It's the glow of a broken streetlight flickering across a
field of stone tombs.

21: finally plucking the arrow out of my chest and seeing
the stretch of the sun's rays
reaching out to hold me in an embrace,
its glow, warm like
Tatay's Smile

Nanay

My grandmother runs laps to and from the
simbahan–church
to the *palengke–market,* selling the clothes off her back,
the slippers under her feet,
and necklaces laced with *Sampaguitas* to buy
a fistful of rice and slices of meat the size of two fingers.
She divides food evenly amongst her four children and
husband and
leaves three grains of rice for herself. She says
the Father, Son, and Holy Spirit are enough to fill her
stomach
with the Faith to carry all of the weight of her
family's survival.
The pressure pushes down on her calves just as much as
the Earth's
gravity presses down on her shoulders.
She lifts her children up with nothing but a 6th
grade certificate,
a bag of clothes to sell, and a pig pen in the backyard.
Simplé lang ang buhay namin, pero masaya–
Our life is just simple, but happy, she says with a
tired smile with three twinkles of light in her eyes.

But even when her knees buckle and her legs quake,
or when her chest clutches and her heart aches,
she digs out the overgrown weeds of her past,
plants seeds in the present,
so they can bloom into a perfume of *Sampaguitas* in
the wind,
praying to the Father, Son, and Holy Spirit that
maybe tonight,
she'll be able to fill her stomach.

Taller and Higher

4

I have a dream of the time I slept over my friend's house
She groaned at the obnoxious buzz of the alarm
Her mom gently rolled her out of her princess-themed bed
She asked if she could sleep over my house next week.
I didn't know how to tell her that I didn't have one.
I didn't know how to tell her that my daily alarm clock consists of
the shouting and hollering the elderly lady that my mother cares for makes.
My mother does not roll me out of bed.
She nudges and hovers above the ancient ottoman where I lay.
She looks at me steadily with tired, sleepless eyes.
A finger pressed against her lips. *Shhh...*
The old lady hates children in her home.
I nod and say "sure!" to my friend anyways and hope
she forgets.

6

I wake up 5 minutes too late. The Metro Bus leaves at 5:50,
it is already 6:30
I hold on to my father so tightly I can hear the gears in his
head whirring, and cranking out
vocabulary words he learned at school
His strained eyes press together so hard he could see
equations embedded
on his eyelids and like a tree in harsh winds, he sways
from side to side.
I look up at my dad and say *"sorry"*

My father smiles and whispers *"it's okay,"* as if he didn't
have enough energy to generate a voice
A shiny red car suddenly stops in front of us, the gust of its
powerful engine suffocates our
breath
It's my friend in the back seat, she rolls her window down,
scowls at me in pity.
Ashamed, I turn my tired eyes away, and hope that my
worn-out uniform would magically look new.
She never asks to sleep over again.

10

I fall asleep on a couch at the Goodwill.
A loud plop and clattering metal startle me awake.
It's a girl dropping off boxes of princess-themed bedroom
decorations for donation.
I look at her and recognize her familiar eyes and freeze.
She stares back at me and drills shame into my skull
She leaves without uttering a word, but her disgusted eyes
paint a whole novel of her thoughts.
I retreat to my parents who are standing by the door, with
a smile too big to fit their jaded eyes.

18

I realize that while my eyes were closed
My mother strained to keep hers open, holding an
entrance to a collapsing cave
While my mind was at rest
My father's raced infinite marathons in between earning
good grades for this week's quiz and
 earning enough money for this week's dinner
Till now, I cannot comprehend how they were able to

keep their systems running with broken circuits
But I do know that the electricity that runs through their
blood is a vision of a greater future.
This power and drive to push beyond limits unknown,
to venture to foreign lands owning nothing but a heavy
accent, love, and a vision for more.
This energy buzzes and hums inside my mother's eyes, my
father's mind.
Constantly thinking about me, about them, and about us.
Gears restlessly whirring and pounding through late
nights and early mornings,
an unstoppable source, pumping from their hearts.
Zapping their brains every time tears fell, arguments broke,
or will-power evaporated
To remind them of their vision to go taller and higher from
where they started before.
It took me a while to understand this,
but now

I am 18
It's 6:30.
I rise out my bed, walk the floors of a house built on heavy
accents, love, and a vision for more.
I pass by the sound of my parents sleeping peacefully
behind their bedroom door.
I grab boxes of worn-out school clothes, slightly yellowed
at the collars, withered at the ends of the skirts.
I drive up to the Goodwill donation center, see a young
boy in a hand-me-down uniform resting
upon an ancient leather ottoman blanketed in dust

18

I learn that that little boy is my younger brother's friend.
He comes over to play, fascinated by video games and
LEGO bricks.
My younger brother asks him if he can come over to his
home one of these days,
The little boy hesitates to answer, so I step in and
offer snacks.
He looks relieved, hoping that my brother will forget.

18

I yearn for the day where immigrant families don't have to
carry the burden of a collapsing cave
where every immigrant child can hear the sounds of their
parents' well-deserved rest,
proudly have their friends come over to play,
and greet days with a buzzing *"hello"* from the thudding
energy in their chest
determined to jumpstart broken circuits, burn boundary
lines, and project the brightness of the
world ahead.

This energy buzzes and hums inside my blood.
They say I inherited my mother's eyes and my
father's smile,
but I like to say that I inherited their hearts.
Their loud, electrifying hearts
an unstoppable source beating from my chest,
zapping my brain every time tears fell, arguments broke,
or will-power evaporated
to remind me of *their* vision, *my* vision, to stand taller and
higher than before

Education

My mother once told me,
*"They can take everything away from you, but they cannot
take away your education"*
and I stood there with salty tears and salty snot racing
down my face
As my mother tried to wash off the glue and sand the
kindergarten bullies poured on my head
fully knowing that I wouldn't "tattle-tale" on them because
I didn't know how to.
And no, I don't mean that I was too nice to throw them
under the bus,
(because believe me I would've)
I mean, I didn't know how to
because my lips still kissed the sandy shores of Philippine
beaches
and my tongue was still superglued to my native language:
I just didn't know how to

That day, I asked to be homeschooled,
but my mother looked at me dead in the eyes and said:
*"They can take everything away from you, but they cannot
take away your education"*

That was the first phrase I learned in English
and I spit it out at bullies with pride.

When they snipped my bangs with safety scissors and I
took one look at them and said,
*"You can take everything away from me, but you cannot take
away my education"*

In 5th grade,
my teacher told my parents to send me back to the
Philippines because I was too behind,
so, I started reading books meant for kids in the 8th grade
and I went to her desk and said,
"You can take everything away from me, but you cannot take
away my education"

In 11th grade,
My counselor told me that my character wasn't something
the UC schools were looking for,
 so when I was accepted to all UC schools,
I marched to her office and said,
"You can take everything away from me, but you cannot take
away my education"

In my third year of college,
I stared into a mirror and saw eyes rimmed with red,
circles darker than my own thoughts.
The pressure was quicksand
and the stress was an endless sea of glue I was sinking in.
Gasping for air, I looked into that mirror and told myself,
"nothing can be taken away from you because you have
an education"

This phrase has evaporated the grains of sand on my lips
into fresh waves of English words
it has melted the glue on my tongue into the smooth
poems of Maya Angelou

Telling me that I am a phenomenal woman
how I can sing of freedom

how I can still rise despite my circumstances because of
the gift of education

You see, we too often hear stories of the song of freedom,
and the bird still being able to rise
 amidst the glue and sand
but nobody talks about the 690,000 birds who cannot
confidently say:
*"you can take everything away from me, but you cannot take
away my education"*
We call them DREAMERS, but nobody should ever only
dream about getting an education

Education is a fundamental human right
and these bullies may splatter your wings with tar and
glass
They may snip your feathers
Tell you to go back to where you belong
Tell you that you do not fit into their standards
and they will want you to whimper in the corner with salt
and snot racing down your face

But no matter what shore your lips touch,
no matter what continent your tongue is from
We will rise
We will sing of freedom
We will continue to be phenomenal
and together, with no fear, we will say:

*"You can take everything away from us, but you cannot take
away our education"*

Love Languages

My family does not say *I love you*
at least not in person
I can't remember the last time I kissed my Mother on the
cheek or
hugged my Uncle goodbye
My Father patted me on the head when I graduated
and my Brother gave me a thumbs up––on Facebook
My Ninang shares her Netflix account.
My Lolo washes my car and gives me a smile he's been
practicing in the mirror for weeks
My Lola gives me clothes that do not fit her and always
makes sure to
share my most recent profile picture

When my brother and I were abroad,
we called our parents and they muttered *I love you* before
hanging up
quick, awkward, and rushed
like trying to steal from a CVS without pockets
It was as if their tongues did not know how to properly roll
the words out of their mouths
and like a fish who found the shore before the sea,
this phrase didn't seem to know how to survive in
their mouths;
an environment they've never been in

gasping,
wheezing,

lost.

I choke on air as soon as
these words ring in my ears.
After years of being submerged in a sea of
head pats, thumbs ups
and reaffirming Facebook posts

I choke on the clumsy music of their voices.
An album that I've listened to for 22 years, sounds like a
new record
spinning, spinning, spinning.

I wish I had captured that moment in my voicemail,
so I could play it when I run my next marathon
a symphony of love and lightening,
flooding my heart with the familiar music of a
love language
that is my own.

Lola

Lola is like an ocean
Every wrinkle on her skin a
gentle wave in the sea I wish I could swim in,
so perhaps she can remember me—
the icy dewdrop who fell from a flustered cloud,
rushing to melt into her warm, cerulean arms
turning chilling memories into
mossy anchors, abandoned treasure chests,
buried under salt and sand

She knows I have a tendency to drift to the deep end
without knowing how to swim

She holds my frozen face in her loving hands, tells me—
there's a thin line between drowning and diving,
you just need a stronger heart for the latter.

Her mind is endless like these waters—wide and wise,
clear on the surface,
yet so mysterious underneath the bright twinkle in her
eyes
Her memories and daydreams float calmly in the
depths below,
old treasures she's forgotten and won't be able to show
What I know about her in my lifetime is little,
yet what she knows about me expands around the Earth
Every time I brush against her soft waves,
I melt into her arms all over again
Her heart—welcoming, wonderful, warm,
a gentle cradle after a thunderous storm

Now, Lola is both the ocean and the sun sinking into the sea,
She dives into the shimmering deep ends with a strong heart,
reuniting with her daydreams and memories

Kain Na

I miss the smell of sizzling garlic in the morning,
fried with stale, white rice from two nights before,
showing me that old things can always be revived
with a little heat from the heart and little time on
the hands.

My Tita stands over the stove with a hunched back,
jiggly arms, and no teeth.
She puts out paper plates from restaurants unknown
with mismatched napkins
and utensils in plastic wrap.

She flips the eggs, fries the *skinless longganisa,*
while watching *Umagang Kayganda.*
I drag my brother out of bed,
toothbrush in my mouth, backpack in my hand
we are late and both of us have grumbling stomachs

Kain na!—Time to eat!

We break the yolk on a
beautiful bed of garlic rice with
juicy pieces of sweet *longganisa,*
but scarf it down too fast

there's never enough time to enjoy
a morning meal in America.

Sarap!—Delicious! We thank her.

Tita asks me if we want *baon—packed lunch,*
We solemnly look at her toothless frown and
wrinkled forehead.
A Pilipino Tita's love language is always food,
but we refuse.

Garlic rice and sweet sausages
are unacceptable in America.
They laugh at our breath and pinch their noses in America.

We take our pre-made packs of peanut butter and jelly.
A meal less delicious, but sadly more accepted in America.

Every day we are split between
protecting our pride in America
and protecting Tita's heart at home.

One day, she stops offering *baon.*
She leaves the rice stale and cold
and puts out our sandwiches on the table,
barren of mismatched paper plates and plastic cutlery
from restaurants unknown

I regret breaking the love language of someone
who just wanted to fill our bellies with garlic rice that
warmed our hearts and satisfied our tongues,
just so we could blend in with America.

Muscle Memory

How many years have you spent practicing your smile?
Placing a goniometer to every cheek and dimple,
measuring-tape at the bottom of your lip,
making sure every Student of the Month ceremony and
Academic Celebration matches
picture perfectly

Your parents say, "the more you practice, the faster it
becomes muscle memory,"
so you memorize the multiplication tables up to x20,
all the states and their capitals,
every planet and their moons,
scrubbed every dish and spoon until they
sparkled in your happy reflection

eventually, muscle memory becomes self-conditioning
like the way you conditioned yourself to *not* be sad,
to *not* cry.
You are too busy translating documents, taking care of
your pseudo-children siblings, and bringing home
pristine report cards.

So you swallow your tears and start to multiply,
recite the planets, the capitals and the moons
anything to distract yourself from
your mother's angry voice or
your dad's stern stare
or the sad eyes in the mirror that
glistens and glares

You learn to accept firecracker words that make
your blood boil or burn your skin and tell yourself
they probably weren't meant to be said and
you shouldn't be so sad or mad
you should be grateful,
you should be happy and smile

because muscle memory tells you that
you are your parents' happiness,

so shape up.

Singe your tear ducts close because
this crying stuff wasn't a part of the show
Tears were not part of the picture-perfect face displayed in your
grand museum of accomplishments and flawless Facebook posts
there are no mistakes in this script
no wrong angle or costume change
no tears or rebellion,
teenage transitions or adolescent change

You are the star actress in the show *The Good Daughter*
the role model, the idol
the one that every parent wants,
every sibling dreads and
every child aspires to be

Respect your elders, even if they're in the wrong
don't stand up, sit down.
Know your place and nod your head.

Stay calm, collected and neutral
like the Big Sister you're supposed to be,
listen to others even if your voice gets lost in their
yelling and stomping because
you are a daughter and
you cannot taint your family tree
Know your roles,
they should all be
muscle memory.

Pilipinx-American

Pilipinx-American is an oxymoron.
Two contradictions forced together like
opposite ends of a magnet.
It seems as though I cannot carry one
without letting go of the other--
I wonder how I could possibly hold
two cultures that seem to repel
I need one to thrive,
I need the other to survive.

Finding Home

At first, finding a home in a hostile land sounds a lot like
Stockholm Syndrome.
I cannot comprehend whether I am just too comfortable
living
in the belly of a beast or if I've actually found a community
of survivors deep in its pits, willing to share stories,
light a campfire, perhaps even brainstorm ways to
cut through the thick skin of the monster, holding
us hostage.

The beast called America silently sleeps,
his gurgling belly shakes survivors' bones.
But we all hold on to each other,
cook our favorite foods and
keep the fire burning in our hearts,
an ember that glows in the darkest crevices of this
demon's spine.
a flame that not even the beast can extinguish with his icy
breath

They say home is where the heart is, and my heart lies in
my people.
I feel the sun glowing in their skin and the
glistening of dewy leaves in their eyes.
Their voices are drums that lead me to my lost ancestors,
to the scrambled bits of history buried in this monster's past.
We've gathered mountains of pages of long-lost texts and
stitch them together with thin threads of memories we've
stuffed in our pockets, hoping to
revive the story of our people who have battled this beast
long before we even tried.

Sunsets

I love the way the sun melts into oceans,
creating oil paintings on blank canvas skies
the way the moon strokes shadows of trees,
extracts the green out of leaves
showing us that there is beauty in the warmth that leaves
and the cold that kisses our cheeks,
leaving a rosy goodbye

Spangled

In this small foreign body
under this heavy, twisted tongue
is the fighting spirit of
three golden stars and a sun
still gleaming with pride
even if
fifty stars and thirteen stripes try to strangle it

Halo-Halo

To the boy who called me a mutt:

I think you mean to say,
I'm a concoction of all things sweet and familiar.
I'm the satisfying crunch of ice at the bottom of your cup
and the mush of *munggo beans*
shoveled under the ashes Japanese imperialism left behind.
Where there was fire, there were also hills of snowflakes
soaked
in splashes of canned milk, cooling the sticky sweat
sizzling under the Philippine sun.
I'm soft and green *gulaman,* harvested from the oceans
that the Spanish and the Americans
ripped apart
like how they ripped *all of us* apart like threads of *jackfruit,*
lost and drowning in murky waters, using *minatamis na*
saging as lifesavers, they struggle to
keep afloat
I struggle to save these threads and give them a warm
home but
Leche Flan gets in the way.

Leche Flan's slumped softly atop and thinks it's still siesta
in Barcelona.
So there he stays afloat on the beautiful *Ube Halaya*
She's grown from the rich soil my ancestors toiled
and watered,
harvested with strong hands and sweet smiles.
Even when she is sliced apart, she only reveals love and a
purple heart.

But now she carries the weight of the colonial world--
sinking,

                sinking

                                sinking

down

navigating through this confusing cup and occasionally
giving *ube ice cream* a kiss on the cheek,
reminding her of the roots that make her whole.

To the boy who called me a mutt:

My layers and flavors are too rich for you to swallow.
You might find me confusing, but my culture is a sweet
delicacy that your tastebuds cannot
afford.
I'm not your grandmother's apple pie or your father's root
beer float,
I'm a dynamic mix of history,
mix of ancestry,
mix of survival,
mix of power,
mix of revolution,
mix of justice,

And yes, I am still figuring out the mix of things in this
cultural *halo-halo*
and you can call me a mutt,
an inbred,
a disaster,
a mud-blood

But I have felt the rich soil my ancestors toiled and watered in my palms,

I have felt the strong hands and sweet smiles that keep me rooted in my homeland,

even when you slice me apart, I will only show love and a purple heart,

I will still carry the weight of this colonial world, but I rise, rise

rise with my people

who, in all their *halo-halo* layers are,

fully,

wholly, and

unapologetically Pilipinx

NOTES

———

HISTORY

FERDINAND MAGELLAN

History books tell us that Ferdinand Magellan is credited for "discovering" the Philippines. However, Indigenous people already inhabited the Philippine islands long before Magellan set sail. Lapu-Lapu is regarded as a national hero for killing Magellan at the Battle of Mactan.[32] However, current historical analysis shows that the Battle of Mactan was not so much a heroic battle in defense of the Philippines but a heated rivalry between two Philippine powers: Lapu-Lapu and Rajah Humabon.[33] Magellan just so happened to get in the way of the tension.

---

32 "History of the Philippines," California State University, Bakersfield, accessed July 12, 2020.

33 Justin Umali, "Was Lapu-Lapu Really That Heroic?" *Esquire*, accessed August 28, 2020.

A *Kampilan* is a traditional Pilipino weapon that is rumored to have been used by Lapu-Lapu when killing Magellan. [34]

RIZAL

José Rizal is a physician, poet, and author. He advocated for the Philippines to be a province of Spain. Despite this, he is still regarded as a Philippine national hero for his influential novels. Rizal also was fond of young people and their potential to reshape the future of the Philippines.[35] Though he is personally not my favorite Philippine heroic figure (due to him selling off Philippine independence), I do love one of his most famous lines *"Ang kabataan ang pag-asa ng bayan"* which is translated roughly in the end lines of this piece as golden shovel.

GOLDEN SHOVEL: ANDRÉS BONIFACIO

Andres Bonifacio is another Philippine national hero, nationalist, and revolutionary. He was the founder of the revolutionary Katipunan society in the Philippines which advocated for complete independence from the Spanish.[36] This piece is inspired by his poem "Pag-Ibig sa Tinubuang Lupa," which translates to "Love of Country."

4 JULY 1776

July 4, 1776 is American Independence Day.

---

34 Ron Kosakowski, "Kampilan," *Traditional Filipino Weapons*, accessed August 28, 2020.

35 The Editors of Encyclopaedia Britannica, "Jose Rizal: Filipino Political Leader and author," *Encyclopedia Britannica*, accessed November 26, 2020.

36 The Editors of Encyclopaedia Britannica, "Andres Bonifacio: Filipino Political Leader," *Encyclopedia Britannica*, accessed November 26, 2020.

"Birth of our nation" is a reference to the racist movie "Birth of a Nation."

4 JULY 1902

Spain surrendered the Philippines to the United States in the 1898 Treaty of Paris for $20 million. The Pilipino people were betrayed and angry and thus rebelled against this handover. This led to the bloody Philippine-American War in 1899. President Teddy Roosevelt declared military "victory" over the Philippines on July 4, 1902. Resistance outside of Luzon lasted until 1913. An estimated 200,000 Pilipinos died in the process.[37]

4 JULY 1946

July 4, 1946 is the day the United States formally recognized the independence of the Republic of the Philippines. This day is also commemorated as "Filipino-American Friendship Day." Despite this guise of "independence," the United States still holds a strong influence on the Philippine government. [38]

3 JULY 2020

July 3, 2020 is the day that Philippine President Rodrigo Duterte signed the widely opposed "Anti-Terrorism Act of 2020" as an official law. This law contains provisions that target activists and human rights defenders.[39]

---

37   Becky Little, "The Surprising Connection Between the Philippines and the Fourth of July," *National Geographic,* accessed July 1, 2020.

38   "Republic Day," *Official Gazette*, Republic of the Philippines, accessed July 4, 2020.

39   Jim Gomez, "Philippine President Signs Widely Opposed Anti-Terror Law," *The Washington Post*, accessed July 3, 2020.

MARIA LORENA BARROS

Maria Lorena Barros was a University of the Philippines scholar, poet, activist, and revolutionary militant. She organized the all-women activist group Malayang Kilusan ng Bagong Kababaihan (Makibaka). However, Dictator Ferdinand Marcos charged her with subversion after suspending the writ of habeas corpus in 1971. She was able to escape to the countryside where she continued to do activist organizing among peasants. She was arrested in 1973 but escaped after a year. She rejoined a political underground rebellion movement to dethrone the Marcos regime. Marcos announced a ₱35,000 reward for her capture. Barros was captured in 1976 by constabulary soldiers. She was seriously wounded, so her captors offered medical attention in return for information about the rebellion. Barros refused, saying she wanted to die with her beliefs. She was shot in the nape of the neck at only twenty-eight years old.[40]

RED

This poem references the Trail of Tears or the Indian Removal Act of 1831.

WHITE

This poem references the anti-Pilipino riots that took place in Yakima, Washington; Wenatchee, Washington; and Watsonville, California.[41]

"Little Brown Brother" was a term coined by William Howard Taft that was eventually used by Americans to refer

---

40 Bantayog ng mga Bayani."Barros, Ma. Lorena M.," *The Nameless*, The Project Nameless Collective, accessed July 21, 2020.

41 Trevor Griffey, "The Ku Klux Klan and Vigilante Culture in Yakima Valley," The Seattle Civil Rights and Labor History Project, The University of Washington, 2007.

to Pilipinos. William Howard Taft was the first American Governor-General of the Philippines and the 27th President of the United States.

ODE TO THE MANONGS

"Manongs" translates to "older man" and refers to a group of 100,000 Pilipino farmworkers who immigrated to the United States. The manongs of Delano, CA, faced harsh and unfair working conditions and wages. Eventually, Pilipino labor leaders like Philip Vera Cruz and Larry Itliong convinced the Mexican farmworkers to fight against these conditions, which led to the famous Delano Grape Strike of 1965.[42]

The "clap" at the end of the poem refers to the "unity clap" which originated with the United Farm Workers as a way to bridge the language gap between the Latino and Pilipino farmworkers. The clap begins slowly then gradually gets faster and faster.

KNOW HISTORY, KNOW SELF—DELANO 1965

September 8, 1965 is the day the Agricultural Workers Organizing Committee (AWOC) began the strike against the Delano grape growers. AWOC demanded equal pay and better working conditions. Pilipino leaders, Larry Itliong and Philip Vera Cruz, made an agreement with Cesar Chavez and Dolores Huerta, the leaders of the Mexican American National Farmworkers Association.[43]

---

42 Dennis Arguelles, "Remembering the Manongs and the Story of the Filipino Farm Worker Movement," National Parks Conservation Association, May 25, 2017.

43 Dennis Arguelles, "Remembering the Manongs and the Story of the Filipino Farm Worker Movement," National Parks Conservation Association, May 25, 2017.

KNOW HISTORY, KNOW SELF—INTERNATIONAL HOTEL 1968-1977

The International Hotel or "I-Hotel" was a low-income residence that mostly housed Pilipino seniors in San Francisco. From 1968 to 1977, the landlords of the I-Hotel tried to evict all of the residents to build a parking lot. The tenants organized mass protests to resist eviction. The protest spread among the San Francisco community, which created a multi-racial alliance. Though tenants were able to keep the landlords from demolishing the I-Hotel at first, a violent police riot plowed down 3,000 protesters on August 4, 1977. The original building was demolished in 1979, but, thanks to community efforts, the I-Hotel was rebuilt in 2005 to provide low-income senior housing once again.[44]

GOLDEN SHOVEL: DR. DAWN MABALON

Dr. Dawn Bohulano Mabalon is the first Pinay to earn a Ph.D. in American History from Stanford University. Her dissertation was published by Duke University Press as *Little Manila is in the Heart: The Making of the Filipina/o American Community in Stockton, California*. The book, which serves as inspiration for this poem, examines the Pilipinx-American community in Stockton, California and argues that Pilipinx immigrants and their descendants created a unique ethnic identity. Mabalon's work contributes to our understanding of the struggle of identity among immigrant and ethnic communities. [45]

---

44 "Seeds of the Community," Manilatown Heritage Foundation, manilatown.org, accessed August 1, 2020.

45 "The Passing of Dr. Dawn Bohulano Mabalon," San Francisco State University, August 23, 2018.

CULTURE

BALIKBAYAN BOX

I'm an expert in all things concerning a Balikbayan Box mostly because it was my mother's business for several years. "Balikbayan" literally translates to "to go back home." A Balikbayan Box is a simple cardboard box that usually comes in two sizes (regular and jumbo). They're filled with gifts and goods like canned goods, clothes, towels, toothpaste, toys, bags, etc. They're usually sent from abroad by immigrant families or overseas workers. They are then shipped to the homes of their families in the Philippines. [46]

GLUTATHIONE

Glutathione is a strong antioxidant with anti-melanogenic properties. It has been heavily marketed as a skin-whitening agent in the Philippines. Glutathione is administered primarily through IV or pills. However, it has been integrated in many lotions, soaps, body washes, make-up, sunscreen, etc. The popularity of glutathione in the Philippines is an echo to the colorism that is deeply ingrained in Pilipino culture.[47]

PARÓL

A paról is a traditional Pilipino lantern typically in the shape of a star. The first paról is believed to be made by a man named Francisco Estanislao in 1908 using a traditional star design. It is believed that these lanterns were used to light

46 Daleasis, "Balikbayan Boxes: Symbol of Homesickness, Colonial History, and Family," Bayanihan Foundation Worldwide, October 27, 2018.

47 Sidharth Sonthalia et al, "Glutathione for Skin Lightening: a Regnant Myth or Evidence-Based Verity?" *Dermatology practical & conceptual* 8, no.1 (January 31, 2018): 15-21. DOI: 10.5826/dpc.0801a04.

dark streets during the traditional "Simbang Gabi" or Mass at Night during Christmas. It is derived from the Spanish word "farol," meaning "lantern" or "light." Typical paróls are made with bamboo sticks, paper, and cellophane. More traditional, sturdier paróls are made of windowpane oysters and other translucent shells. [48]

PINAYISM

Is a term coined by Allyson Tintiangco-Cubales and Jocyl Sacramento in their article "Practicing Pinayist Pedagogy." According to Tintiangco-Cubales and Sacramento, Pinayism is "a theoretical framework addressing the social, political, and economic struggles of Pinays."[49] Tintiangco-Cubales and Sacramento also note that Pinayism is rooted in Pinayist pedagogy, which is founded on two things: "1) teaching and learning critical Pinay studies with the central purpose to develop the capacity of Pinays to confront global, local, and personal problems that face them and their community; and 2) mentoring, reproducing, and creating a community of Pinayists."[50]

BAYANIHAN

Bayanihan literally translated to "being a town." It's used to exemplify the spirit for unity, friendship, and community. Traditionally, bayanihan derives from the act of relocating a

---

48 Kevyno Tampino, "The Hands that Craft Stars from Seashells: A Look at the History and Artistry that Goes into each Filipino *Parol*," *Spot*, December 25, 2018.

49 Allyson Tintiangco-Cubales & Jocyl Sacramento, *Practicing Pinayist Pedagogy*, Amerasia Journal, 35:1 (2009).DOI: 10.17953/amer.35.1.98257024r4501756.

50 Allyson Tintiangco-Cubales & Jocyl Sacramento, *Practicing Pinayist Pedagogy*, Amerasia Journal, 35:1 (2009).DOI: 10.17953/amer.35.1.98257024r4501756.

family's home by gathering dozens of community volunteers to lift the home using bamboo poles to another location. This is typically celebrated later on through a fiesta.[51]

REVOLUTION AND REVELATION

DARE TO STRUGGLE, DO NOT BE AFRAID
Common activist/protest chant translated from "Makibaka Huwag Matatakot."

TO ZARA: TOGETHER WE RISE, KASAMA
Zara Alvarez was a human rights activist, paralegal, and member of the Negros Integrated Health Program. She was shot in Bacolod City on August 17, 2020, by "unidentified perpetrators." Zara is the latest victim of the extrajudicial killings of the Duterte regime. This poem is an elegy that echoes the public letter she wrote to her family while she was held as a political prisoner: *"Still, one voice is a noise, but more voices is a voice of freedom, soon we realize, everybody are singing the song of the people, taking a stand to end political persecution and demanding justice to all victims of human rights violations. Time will come that no amount of fear can stop us in cultivating everybody's freedom."*

TO THE LUMAD: THERE IS POWER IN THE YOUTH WHO DREAM
This poem speaks to the unjust and inhumane attacks and killings of Indigenous peoples in the Philippines. This poem specifically describes the experiences of the Lumad

---

51 Samly, "Bayanihan: Communal Spirit in Philippines," *AsianCustoms.eu,* accessed August 20, 2020.

populations in Mindanao, Philippines. The Lumad have resisted against land confiscations, logging, and mining on Indigenous, ancestral lands.

LIBERTY IN SHACKLES

Reference a picture of the Statue of Liberty and pay close attention to the shackles on her ankles. This may be a remnant of the original intention behind the gift of Lady Liberty. The Statue of Liberty was originally given as a gift to commemorate abolition and the liberation of slaves.[52]

BAYAN KO?—MY COUNTRY?

This poem is based off of the work of my ancestor/relative José Corazón de Jesús or "Huseng Batute." José Corazón de Jesús composed the poem/song "Bayan Ko" in the late 1920s when Pilipino activists were calling for independence from the imperial United States. It was set to music by Constancio de Guzman during the struggle against the Marcos dictatorship in the 1980s. In his poem, de Jesús talks about Spanish colonization and US colonization. He compares the Philippines to a free bird once independence is achieved.

---

52   Gillian Brockell, "Statue of Liberty was Created to Celebrate Freed Slaves not Immigrants," *The Washington Post*, May 23, 2019.

ACKNOWLEDGMENTS

Poetry is often thought to be the product of the self, but to me, poetry is the product of the community. I have been so blessed to be surrounded by people who have poured their relentless love, support, generosity, and appreciation for my work and passions. I am privileged and ever so lucky for my family and my friends, classmates, and co-workers who have become a part of my family along the way. I'd like to take this time to individually recognize my family and community for their love.

Dad: I know you much prefer watching the History Channel and measuring medications in milligrams than reading poetry. I've always found it funny that writing was supposedly your "weakest" school subject, yet your handwriting, which I did not inherit, is so beautiful. You may not understand everything in this book, but I know you will try. You will nod your head, smile, say, "Good job Ate Kai!" and go on about your day.

Mom: You've been my number one fan since the day I decided to pick up a pencil and start writing. You say I got it all from you, and for the first time aloud, I must say that I agree. Thank you for seasoning me with your tough love. You've taught me the importance of generosity, grace, and kindness. I take every one of your Facebook posts about me to heart even though neither of us ever really show it. You've trained my wings to be strong and powerful. I can't wait to finally use them and fly. Thank you for being the loudest in every audience and the first to clap at every performance.

Lola and Lolo: I am learning how to read both of your love languages. The more I observe and analyze them, the more my heart swells in happiness and appreciation for both of you. Salamat po for doing your part in advising me and teaching me with your wisdom and knowledge. Even though both of your diabetes management skills stress me out, I do it out of love.

Nanay and Tatay: Though we may be apart, I know my heart is closer to both of you than ever. Nanay, all your voicemails and surprise messages are precious to me. I miss your warmth, laughter, and hugs. Every time I come home from work and shower immediately, or go to bed with wet hair, I already hear your voice telling me about the consequences. Tatay, I know you're smiling with your eyes crinkled from up above.

And to my pre-sale supporters, this book would not come to life without your trust and belief in me:
In Alphabetical order

Ebony Alamillo: My fellow bookworm and friend, I'm glad to still be in touch from afar even after all these years. I'm proud of who you've become. We've come a long way since burgundy uniforms and khaki pants. Stay authentic, bookish, and proud.

Arlo Alegre: Kasamang Arlo! May your nails stay painted, your hair dyed, and your revolutionary fervor ignited. You are the best organizer out there! I honestly don't know how you balance so many things at once. Also, do you want to build a snowman?

Justine Asas: They say only the most attractive people are named Justine. I'm sorry we never got to go to California Donuts together after your travels from afar. Despite it all, I can feel your friendship all the way from Chicago.

Beatrice Maron Avancena: Fashion icon and SPACE queen, you are a beautiful, bubbly spirit. We need more of you in this world. I'm incredibly proud of you for all that you've accomplished at UCLA. You are talented, gorgeous, and so passionate. May your wardrobe one day exchange for mine.

Maybellene Averion: Tita May, I look up to you and hope to one day be as fulfilled and successful as you. You are generous, kind, and compassionate about everyone around you, whether it be your co-workers, classmates, or friends.

Clarissa Ayala: Salamat for entrusting me in delivering this work of poetry to your doorstep! My heart is so full knowing that I have a supporter like you.

Susana Barajas: I will never forget all the times we shared laughter, frustrations, Starbucks, cookies, and all of the above. Your tenacious, headstrong, and empathetic spirit is something the OT world needs. I'm glad we both started work together; I would not have wanted it any other way. You've been through so much in your lifetime, and it has only made you more resilient and strong-willed. One day, we'll work together again as OTs and "jack" everyone up in whatever workplace we end up in.

Angelica Barakat: When we met, we were both still lost in a major we weren't entirely sure about. I'm glad we've both found our ways and never have to take another wretched Shakespeare or Anglo-Saxon literature class ever again. Keep being the amazingly sustainable advocate you are!

Vivian Beene: Ate Vivian, thank you for being so patient and kind. The Pilipino Alumni Association would not stand as tall and proud without you carrying it on your shoulders. Your dedication to UCLA students and your naturally nurturing soul is admirable and praise-worthy. I look up to you as a mentor, colleague, and friend. I appreciate everything you do.

Marisol Belleza: Tita Marisol, you are a young, dainty, and gentle soul. I hope to one day have your confidence on the dance floor and to retain your youthful, joyous spirit.

Angelica Bernabe: Tita Angelica, I'm rooting for you on the sidelines! You've done a wonderful job raising my two wonderful cousins. I treasure all the moments we shared together when I was still a child.

Tati G. Bongalon: Tita Tati, you've always been so thoughtful, generous, and kind. Thank you for looking after me and my brother and for supporting us throughout all of our milestones. I'll cherish every photo you take of us and every memory we've shared together.

Anabella and Paul Butcon and Family: Tita Anabella and Tito Paul, thank you for always taking care of us. From making sure we are fed, from helping my mom manage crazy events, and being the center of all jokes and laughter (and food).

Yva Kristiana Caces: You've grown so much and have come so far from the little girl I met a decade ago. I'm so proud of who you've become and all that you've accomplished thus far. Your life is just starting and I'm just happy to be a part of it. I can't wait to do all the trips we planned on going on and the adventures we've thought of. It must've taken a lot of crinkle sales to get a copy, so order from @kasamacookies on Instagram so she can get her money back.

Tala Cardenas: Thank you for your generosity and belief in me! It is because of kind people like you that I can live my dreams!

Victoria Castreje: To my fitness guru, dancer babe, and tomato-eating gal, you never cease to blow me away with your hustle and your love for all of your friends. I'm so proud of you and am so happy our paths crossed. Let me be the cheerleader this time. ROOTING FOR YOU!

Sirena Charelian: My Cancer queen! You have the gentlest and kindest soul. You love with a big heart and expect nothing in return. I'm so proud of all you've accomplished and am so grateful for your friendship. I hope to one day reunite and celebrate in our Cancer tears of love.

Yolanda Chavez and Family: You are simply the best! Your positive energy and excitement can light up a whole country. You're always supporting and cheering me on even from afar. I'm so grateful to have met you and your family. You will all be in my heart forever.

Stephanie Chinn: Your laughter is truly contagious. You are a light and joy at work; I don't think I could've done it without you! I look up to you greatly and appreciate you so much. The big sister I never had, truly! Cheers to more crafting and learning!

Aimee Contreras: Thank you for your dedication to our UCLA students and the novel, bright ideas you bring to the table. Being on board with you in PAA is truly a blessing. I aspire to be as strong-willed and passionate as you!

Dr. CoriAndre Crane: Your history lessons and silly stories are things that I have passed on to my students and mentees. You inspired me to reach for higher education and become a passionate and dedicated educator.

Cruz Family: Your New York energy is something I still cannot match. Thank you for always sending your love to the West Coast whenever you can. I know we haven't been able to visit you all as much as you have visited us, but I am certain that will change very soon! I can't wait to hang out with you all.

Cuison Family: Your youthful souls and hearty laughter are things I've missed dearly. I can't wait till we can all get together again and enjoy each other's stories and company. You've always supported and cheered me on since I was just a child. Thank you for always sticking by.

Allene De Castro: Kasamang Allene, I have never met someone so organized, passionate, and headstrong. Thank you for your organizational work and your commitment toward anti-colonialism and fascism. I look up to you!

Pearl Doan: I've always thought that such a beautiful name was such a good fit for such a beautiful soul. You are gentle, kind, and eager to support and help everyone around you. You truly live up to your name. Thank you for being such a jewel.

Victoria Echegaray: Vicky, you are so resilient and determined. Being a daughter, mother, and wife is not an easy job! Despite this, you are still so dedicated to education and being an advocate for children with special needs. You are everything I strive to be!

Estrella Family: Ninang Annie and Tito Jojo, you have been there since the very beginning. You have done a wonderful job raising two smart and talented children. Salamat Po for always encouraging me and sending me all your love throughout my life. I thank the heavens for family like you!

Venice Europa: You made me feel so welcome, seen, and accepted in a new environment. Your sense of humor, genuine care, and love is always a highlight of my day. I'm so excited for the new baby. I hope to one day meet both of your girls and share our love of "Le Petit Elefant."

Idyl Eusebio and Porty: Tita Idyl, you're an amazing mother, daughter, and sister. I'm so proud to have such a spunky cousin like Porty. I can't wait to visit you all in Chicago, watch musicals, and eat exotic foods. Thank you for sending your love from so far away.

Leslie Fabello: Having your support and love is a privilege not many have! It's people like you who inspire my poetry and motivate me to write louder, bolder, and fiercer!

Gaston and Eileen Flores: Okaay Barong/Bamboo Boy, I see you! Your cheerful and energetic yet peculiar and unique personality lights up my day. Thanks for enduring my sarcasm and odd humor. Eileen, I don't know how you handle him, but I commend you for it. I hope you enjoy your very late Christmas gift!

Jasmin Galvez: Kring-Kring! I've always looked up to you and am in awe at your confidence, compassion, and gentle demeanor. You're always so calm, bubbly, and collected. You're going to make a wonderful OT. Thank you for enduring all of my questions about OT!

Lauren Gan: HEY, BAE! I'm always cheering you on, even if it is virtually 98 percent of the time. I never got to tell you this, but you made my high school transition/experience so much better. I don't think I could've endured high school without your humor and friendship. SO PROUD OF YOU!

Alexandro Guerrero: You're truly my best friend to the very end. Thank you for always believing in me, supporting me, and just overall being a great listener and advisor. I'm so glad we'll be able to make more memories in grad school. We've accomplished so much as a team; I can't wait to learn and grow with you! From Bruins to Jumbos!

Jeremy Guiman: You are wise beyond your years! I really wish we met each other in person. Being in a virtual SPACE internship with you was amazing. I was always in total awe of your knowledge and insight. You have a great future ahead of you, and I can't wait to cheer you on as you succeed.

Sahrang G. Han: You have so many talents, can you please lend me some? I wish we got to know each other more in person! Your dedication to the Pilipinx community at UCLA and commitment to serve with your heart is a blueprint of your future. I'm proud to call you my friend!

Ina Ibrado, Fides Cabildo, and Kawin Koh: Tita Ina, Tita Des, and Tito K, thank you for pushing my mom out of her comfort zone and for always encouraging her to be a better version of herself. I'm glad that fate allowed us to become a small family of our own. I cherish all the laughter, drinks, trips, and Chinese checkers games I've had with all of you!

Noor Javidi: What a blessing it is to have you in my life. What a coincidence that you were my student at the English Academy, my co-worker at EOPS, and a fellow Bruin! Wherever life may take you, I know you have the tenacity and will to take on any endeavor you may face. Best of all, you'll do it with a smile.

Donia Javidi: Your radiant positivity and work ethic amazes me. Once you set your mind onto something, you never let it out of sight. You're not only smart, but kind, and that is why I'm so glad to call you my friend. Your endless support and belief in me have motivated me so much. Thank you, Donia!

Emelyn Judge: You have done a splendid job raising Mika. You are an amazing, supportive, and kind mother. I only wish to be half as good a mom as you are! Thank you for supporting Mika in his poetry journey and now his musical endeavors.

Ashley Ku: I'm so glad I sat in front of you on that day in geography class. We made so many memories together just in a matter of sixteen weeks. We wrote our applications, got accepted into schools, hiked miles and miles for extra credit, and created friendships while we're at it. I'm excited to see you succeed and preach your passion for sustainability. I'm so incredibly proud of you!

Eric Koester: Professor Koester, thank you for never giving up on me. I know it took me three tries to get started with NDP and your writer's program. Georgetown University is so blessed to have such a passionate educator in their hands. I can't wait to see where this book takes me.

Chriselle Lee: You are such an amazing Ate to your siblings, daughter to your parents, and partner to your twin flame! I love seeing all of your pets from your pups to your axolotls. You are not only kind and beautiful, but humble and generous. I wish I had an Ate like you! Thanks for always supporting me even from afar.

Jennifer Lerit: Tita Jennifer, thank you for sending your love and support even from Canada. I know the pre-sale package was pricey for out-of-country shipping, yet you are still one of my most relentless cheerleaders. You have a beautiful and kind soul that I know will be instilled in your children too! Salamat po!

Rebecca Lin: Rebecca, I met you when you were this quiet, studious, color guard girl and when I met you again in college, you were this unapologetically stunning and confident dancer. I was shook—but not really, because I saw those moves during Dancentra tryouts. Keep being the beautiful, talented, intelligent, and humble human you are.

Roderick U Lovo-Donan: We've both grown up to be wiser in our experiences. I'm glad we're able to start difficult conversations and thank you for listening and trying to understand. I'm sure the future holds great things for you, Lovo! Keep learning and unlearning.

Paige MacPherson: Girl, I'm so glad our paths aligned! This year has been an emotional rollercoaster, and I'm glad you were on the ride with me. You are a strong-willed, confident, and sassy baddy, and I only hope to be half as amazing as you are. I can't wait to see the future you thriving, travelling, watching T Swift concerts, and probably doing something outdoorsy in the Pacific Northwest. I will forever treasure my Harry Styles calendar.

Rosette Mariano: Tita Rosette, you are so patient, forgiving, and understanding. God gave the perfect mom to Joseph. I know being a mother is not easy, yet you do it so gracefully.

You are beautiful, kind, and gracious. Thank you for always cheering me on.

Sonia Martinez: I will never forget your bubbly and silly personality. Thank you for being as obsessed with One Direction as me. You made sure that I wasn't alone in my unhealthy obsessions with boybands. One day, we will attend their reunion concert as thirty-something-year-olds. I truly can't wait!

Cesar Martinez: I'm so glad you've found a good path to be on. I know life is rough and can get a little crazy, but you still found your way around. You were always such a wise, critical thinker. Never let that change about you! One day, we'll go around debating together as a team again. But for now, let's stick to our Twitter rants.

AR Mateo: You are such a great ally and representative for UCLA students. Dr. Dawn Malabon would be so proud of the hearts you've touched and the students you've been able to support along the way. I'm so glad I performed that day, or else we would've never met!

Loudee, Homer, and Mateo Mercado: Nang Nang and Tito Homer, thank you for allowing me to see the world with you. My eyes and vision have quite literally been stretched because of our memorable and thrilling trips around the globe. Now a new adventure awaits both of you every day. I can't wait to take Mateo Potato on the same trips around the world one day.

Arielle Moscati: Oh, how far we've come! I always think about the day we met while waiting outside of class. Imagine if we never tried to speak to one another?! (It would be a horrible world). Thank goodness we did! Now all the things we dreamt of are becoming reality. I'm so proud of you, Dr. Moscati/Mrs. Moscati-Leahy, mother of cats and reader of books.

Mariel Joy Neri: Kasamang Mariel! Why does it feel like I've met you in person when we've actually never met in real life? I love our exchange of TikToks, our common love for boy bands, and our discussions on anti-colonialism/imperialism, allyship, and smashing the patriarchal capitalist agenda. I can't wait to rally and protest with you!

Lynn O'Connell: Thank you so much for your belief, trust, and support. You've introduced me to a network of people I would've never known. You are one of many sparks that set fire to my poetry journey. You have such a passion for our alma mater, and I wish to carry that on in the future!

Baktash Olomi: I love your calm demeanor and happy -go-lucky personality. You are humble, kind, and a huge ally to the transfer community. I'm so lucky to have organized with you to make a mark in Regents Scholar history! By the way, I still can't believe you have a life-size Shaq in your room.

Rhodora and Jeff Osborne: Tita Lala and Tito Jeff, thank you for always cheering me on even from all the way from Maryland. I thoroughly enjoyed my time there and hope to go back! I miss my sweet little cousins, Julia, Angela, and Grace. You both raised such intelligent, independent, and respectful girls with such blossoming personalities.

Chuck Parcon: Kasmang Chuck, thank you for always reading my poetry even in its first stages. Together, we've learned so much about ourselves through our writing. I'm glad we're able to be so open and engage in tough conversations about our lives, our mistakes, and our experiences. We grow each and every day. Dahan, dahan lang!

Janella Pizarro: I'm a true believer in the fact that the best kind of love and support comes from those we've never met or those we don't know at all! The fact that you were so willing to support me in my book journey without knowing much about me or my work brings tears to my eyes! Thank you for supporting fellow Pilipinx writers. You're absolutely amazing.

Ann Plauzoles: Ann, you've been such a great resource and supporter of mine. You've always believed in me and celebrated my accomplishments and passions. Your dedication to UCLA students and Gold Shield Scholars has truly touched my heart. I wish to one day join Gold Shield and pass on the same mentorship you provided me to someone else. I cherish the UCLA book of history you gave me. Thank you for making me feel like a true Bruin!

Elissa Quon: I still remember the day you approached me after my Java House performance. You are so incredibly kind, humble, and loving to all you meet. You've won and touched the hearts of many. I'm so proud of what we've accomplished, and I can't wait for what the future holds for us. Thanks for always supporting my poetry since day one!

Kira Radstrom: You are an absolute angel of a human being. I'm so glad I sat across from you in Anatomy that day. Not only did I run into one of the most gorgeous creatures in the world, but also the spunkiest, kindest, and dare I say, most unique. You're going to become the perfect nurse. Your grandmother is so proud of you. I can't wait to go on adventures together.

Stella Ramos: Mama Stella! You are the most easy-going, sleepiest, and most gentle human beings I know! You are incredibly kind to everyone you meet. Your presence is calming and reassuring. Thank you for always supporting me and cheering me on since I was a kid!

Patricia Reyes: Ate Tresh, thank you for being so patient when listening to my rants and complaints. You are the kindest and gentlest soul I've ever known. I know transitioning in this new world is no easy feat, yet you've done so with so much grace. Keep being the generous, empathetic being you are; that is what makes you a wonderful nurse.

Kathleen Robeniol: Thanks for finding my jokes funny and appreciating my witty/snarky comments despite our generational gap. I've lost count of all the inside jokes we've generated. It brings me great joy that you're able to connect with me and my poetry and that you allow yourself to be vulnerable and open. Your journey is just beginning, and I can't wait for you to discover and rediscover yourself. I would say to take it step-by-step, but you already take too many of those in a day to my liking. No cap.

Antonio Rodriguez: The Antonio I met in their first year and the Antonio I now know are completely different people. You've really sprung out of your shell, spread your leaves, and bloomed beautifully. I'm so proud that you're unapologetically fierce, proud, and powerful. You've chosen your own way in this path of life and that's all that matters. I believe in you and trust that you will succeed no matter what happens!

Franz Roxas: You've always been so supportive of Pilipinx creatives, business owners, and professionals alike. We grew up and grew old so fast! Seems like only yesterday you tried teaching me how to do the "cup song" from *Pitch Perfect*. I'm so glad we were able to share a portion of our childhood together. I'll treasure those moments forever!

Jade Saffery: You are my twin flame and soulmate! Cancer + Virgo = Forever. We've made so many memories together, from being late to class, struggling to read Old English, getting recruited into a sorority, and struggling to walk up and down the UCLA hills. One day we'll go to all the Disney parks in the world together and dress up as our favorite characters every single time.

Vianca Santos: Pinsan, I love you so much! I know we're far apart but know that I am always praying for your health and success. I'm rooting for you all the way in California. You've adjusted so well for being in the United States for just a short time. I hope to visit you and take you on adventures that would make your mother worry sick!

Vivian Santos: Ate Vivian, you work so hard to make sure your family is safe, happy, and healthy. You are the Ate that everyone aspires to be. I'm so proud of you for striving to do the very best for your family and always putting them first. One day, I hope to be like you!

Teresa Sarte: Thank you for appreciating and investing in my poetry and my dreams. It's because of people like you that there is still so much hope and positivity in this world. Keep shining and spreading your love! Salamat ulit po!

Apple Sepulveda: You are such a wonderful advocate, educator, and ally. You are not afraid to speak up and speak out. You constantly seek ways to learn and improve. You bring a spark of lightning to every institution that has the privilege of having you in their hands. I look up to you and hope to one day follow your footsteps.

Vicente and Jasmin Serrano: Tita Jasmin and Tito Vince, I'm so glad that both of you made your way to each other. You work together so well as a couple and make each other so happy. You two have been such a huge part of my life. You've witnessed me grow every step of the way and not once did you ever doubt my abilities. Thank you so much.

Tiffany Sloan: Thank you for entrusting me with the great job of writing content I am proud of and that you would be interested in reading. It takes a lot to write poetry, but it takes the power of a community to spread the messages within the poetry. Thank you for being a part of that community.

Marina Sobrevinas: You have a fiery, adventurous spirit and the most empathetic heart. Your passions live beyond the realms of a city, state, or country. You are determined to learn from the people you meet, the paths you bike on, and the mountains you climb. I'm determined you'll go up and over any obstacle in your way. (I mean, it won't be hard with those guns.)

Emily Soriano: Emily, I will always remember you as a sweet, bubbly, and kindhearted girl. Middle school was surely rough and a little dramatic, but that never stopped you from being a genuinely compassionate and friendly person. With this attitude ingrained within you, I know you'll get far wherever you go!

Richard and Ben Stinson: Tito Ben and Richard, thank you so much for always cheering me on and taking me in as your own family. Your love and passion for your families and communities inspire me to be more generous, forgiving, and thoughtful to everyone I come across. I'm so proud and happy to have uncles like both of you in my life!

Pauline Tze: It was such a pleasure watching you burst out of your shell and blossom into a relentlessly confident human! You have so much strength and power in your voice. I know you'll use this special and unique quality to educate others about the causes and communities you love and to change the lives of your students.

Jillian Ubando: I'm incredibly proud of you for pursuing a path you are genuinely passionate about. Art brings you so much joy and I want nothing less for you! I'm so excited to hang your artwork on my walls and attend all of your galleries. Stay beautiful, humble, and talented. You are a ray of sunshine to everyone you know!

Grace and Faith Walter: Tita Grace and Ate Faith, your bond inspires me and is proof that the love between a mother and daughter is the strongest of them all! Tita Grace, you've raised a beautifully outspoken and passionate woman. Ate Faith, you've always been wise beyond your years. I'm so proud you're able to question the world, think critically, and develop your own voice.

Becky Wei: I still remember the day you recognized me at B-Caf amongst crowds of people. I was thrilled and shocked that our paths would meet again. Thank you for approaching me that day and re-introducing yourself! I'm so proud of us for making it through UCLA. I can't wait for the day we regroup in our official ceremony. I'm excited for everything the future holds for such a smart and tenacious woman like you! Thank you so much for supporting me!

Jakob Woo-Ming: Hey Zrother! Thanks for always cheering me on whenever you can. I'm so happy that I got to virtually meet such a bright, spirited personality that strives to make everyone smile. You are absolutely killing it every single day! I'm proud of how far you've come.

Maria Zamarripa: You are soft-spoken, patient, and the most understanding person I've ever met. You are such a light and joy to be around; you make it so easy to be your friend. I can't wait for the day we can all go to Disneyland together again in coordinating outfits. You have been such a loyal friend to me for over a decade. I'm excited to see what the future holds for you. I just can't wait to be there to witness your glorious success every step of the way. I'm so grateful for you and your friendship, love you lots!

Elaina Zeng: Elaina! I'm so happy you entered my life when you did. I was pretty miserable in high school until you came along. There wasn't a day where you didn't make me laugh or make sure I cheered up when I was down. We would get into the most ridiculous situations and say the most nonsensical things, but it all made sense to us. Keep being the hustling, discount-loving, gorgeous, and intelligent woman you are. You're truly such a special gem in my life. I hope you stick around for much longer!

To my manuscript reviewers:

Ashley Lanuza: You're a wonderfully creative creature. Your passion for literature and writing inspires me every day. *My Heart of Rice* is a legendary masterpiece! Though I'm bummed we never got to truly hang out during college, it's never too late! I hope to see your name on the big screen and The New York Times best seller list one day. Thank you so much for your advice, support, and feedback.

Jazzlynn G. Eugenio Pastor: Thank you for always believing in me since the day I first reached out to you. Your generosity with your time and your willingness to spread the word about my book is an act of unforgettable kindness. Thank you @pinaypages!

Leo Albea: You are truly revolutionizing the way Pilipinx people are represented. You are paving the way for future generations to pursue their creative dreams. One day, I hope that my future children can turn on the TV or watch a movie and see their histories, stories, and faces represented on screen.

Nani Dominguez: Thank you for opening up your platform to me. My short chat with you meant so much. All of our stories resonated with each other and we found so much in common. Thank you for spreading our stories as Pinays. Keep blogging, podcasting, and uncovering your Pinay identity.

Professor Stephen Acabado: Professor Acabado, thank you for leaving a Pilipino mark in the world of anthropology. You are so kind and generous of your time. I remember reaching out to you on a Zoom meeting and you were so willing to support me despite just having met me. I hope to be an educator like you one day!

Professor JoAnna Poblete: As a fellow Pilipino Alumni Association board member and a friend, I just want to say that I look up to you so much! You've made great strides in writing Pilipino histories and educating the next generation of scholars. Thank you for always being an ally and for lending your time and effort towards my book.

Professor Kirby Araullo: Kuya Kirby, without your videos and your lessons, there would've never been a book to begin with. There were days where I would watch your channel for hours! I can proudly say I've watched every single one of your videos. Thank you for making culturally relevant education accessible and understandable. You've made such a huge impact in the world of ethnic studies. I can only hope to be half as good of a mentor and educator as you are!

Kasamang JT: Your poetry is beautiful, invigorating, and inspiring. I've read it twice, word-for-word now. I'm so glad to have found another Kasama who is also a poet. Your work for our community will not go unnoticed. Thank you for organizing, fighting, and writing.

And, lastly,

To You: Thank you for listening to my vulnerability, for learning something new, for taking a small peek into my brain and heart. It is only because of readers like you that I am able to keep writing content to share to the world. Maraming Salamat!

APPENDIX

HISTORY

A Capitol Fourth, "The History of the American Flag." Public Broadcasting Service, accessed July 31, 2020. https://www.pbs.org/a-capitol-fourth/history/old-glory/.

Arguelles, Dennis. "Remembering the Manongs and the Story of the Filipino Farm Worker Movement." National Parks Conservation Association, May 25, 2017. Accessed July 31, 2020. https://www.npca.org/articles/1555-remembering-the-manongs-and-story-of-the-filipino-farm-worker-movement.

Bantayog ng mga Bayani, "Barros, Ma. Lorena M." *The Nameless*, The Project Nameless Collective, accessed July 21, 2020. http://www.nameless.org.ph/barros.

Bonifacio, Andres. "Pag-Ibig sa Tinubuang Lupa'." National Government Portal, accessed November 26, 2020. http://malacanang.gov.ph/7050-andres-bonifacios-pag-ibig-sa-tinubuang-lupa/.

California State University Bakersfield, "History of the Philippines," accessed July 12, 2020, https://www.csub.edu/pacificrim/countryprospectus/history.htm.

Gomez, Jim. "Philippine President Signs Widely Opposed Anti-Terror Law." *The Washington Post*, July 3, 2020. Accessed July 13, 2020. https://www.washingtonpost.com/world/asia_pacific/philippine-president-signs-widely-opposed-anti-terror-law/2020/07/03/f0db4cd8-bd28-11ea-97c1-6cf116ffe26c_story.html.

Griffey, Trevor. "The Ku Klux Klan and Vigilante Culture in Yakima Valley." University of Washington, The Seattle Civil Rights and Labor History Project, 2007. Accessed July 25, 2020. https://depts.washington.edu/civilr/kkk_yakima.htm.

Guthrie, Woody, and New London U. S. Coast Guard Band. "This Land Is Your Land." MENC. Audio. https://www.loc.gov/item/ihas.100010446/.

Henry, Patrick. "Speech to the Second Virginia Convention." St. John's Church in Richmond, on March 23, 1775, Virginia. *Gleeditions*, originally published in *Masterpieces of American Eloquence*, accessed August 18, 2020. www.gleeditions.com/speechtothesecondvirginiaconvention/students/pages.asp?lid=414&pg=4.

Jefferson, Thomas. "The Declaration of Independence." July 4, 1776. Accessed July, 4 2020. https://etc.usf.edu/lit2go/133/historic-american-documents/4957/the-declaration-of-independence/.

Kosakowski, Ron. "Kampilan." *Traditional Filipino Weapons*, accessed August 28, 2020. https://www.traditionalfilipinoweapons.com/shop/kampilan/.

Little, Becky. "The Surprising Connection Between the Philippines and the Fourth of July." *National Geographic*, accessed July 1, 2020. https://www.nationalgeographic.com/news/2016/07/july-4-philippines-independence-day-america-holiday/#close.

Mabalon, Dawn Bohulano. *Little Manila is in the Heart.* North Carolina: Duke University Press Books, 2013.

Manilatown Heritage Foundation. "Seeds of the Community." *Manilatown,* accessed August 1, 2020. https://manilatown.org/about-us/history/.

"Republic Day," *Official Gazette*, Republic of the Philippines. accessed July 4, 2020. https://www.officialgazette.gov.ph/featured/republic-day/about/.

"The Philippine War-Suppressing an Insurrection."National Park Service, last modified February 28, 2015. Accessed January 31, 2021. https://www.nps.gov/prsf/learn/historyculture/the-philippine-war-suppressing-an-insurrection.htm.

The Editors of Encyclopaedia Britannica. "Andres Bonifacio: Filipino Political Leader." *Encyclopedia Britannica*, accessed November 26, 2020. https://www.britannica.com/biography/Andres-Bonifacio.

The Editors of Encyclopaedia Britannica, "Jose Rizal: Filipino Political Leader and author." *Encyclopedia Britannica*, accessed

November 26, 2020. https://www.britannica.com/biography/ Jose-Rizal.

Umali, Justin. "Was Lapu-Lapu Really That Heroic?" *Esquire*, accessed August 28, 2020. https://www.esquiremag.ph/long-reads/features/was-lapu-lapu-really-that-heroic.

Urabe, Toshinao. "Remarks of Ambassador Toshinao Urabe 38th Ship for Southeast Asian Youth Programme (SSEAYP)." Embassy of Japan in the Philippines, November 10, 2020. Accessed August 24, 2020. https://www.ph.embjapan.go.jp/ pressandspeech/speeches/2011/38th%20Ship%20for%20South-east%20Asian%20Youth%20Programme.htm.

Woodie Guthrie and the US Coast Guard Band, "This Land is Your Land," The Library of Congress, February 1940.

CULTURE

Daleasis. "Balikbayan Boxes: Symbol of Homesickness, Colonial History, and Family." Bayanihan Foundation Worldwide, October 27, 2018. Accessed August 2, 2020. https://www.offi-cialgazette.gov.ph/featured/republic-day/about/.

Fisher, William Arms, and Lee Bates, Katharine. "America the Beautiful," Oliver Ditson Company, 1917.

Samly. "Bayanihan: Communal Spirit in Philippines." *Asian Customs.eu*, accessed August 20, 2020. https://asiancustoms.eu/ bayanihan/.

Sonthalia, Sidharth, Abhijeet Kumar Jha, Aimilios Lallas, Geraldine Jain, and Deepak Jhakar. "Glutathione for Skin Lightening: A Regnant Myth or Evidence-Based Verity?" *Dermatology Practical & Conceptual* 8,no.1 (Winter 2018) 15-21. DOI: https://doi.org/10.5826/dpc.0801a04.

"The Passing of Dr. Dawn Bohulano Mabalon," San Francisco State University, August 23, 2018. Accessed February 2, 2021. https://history.sfsu.edu/content/passing-dr-dawn-bohulano-mabalon

Tapnio, Kevyno. "The Hands that Craft Stars from Seashells: A Look at the History and Artistry that Goes into Each Flipino Parol," *Spot*, December 25, 2018. Accessed December 23, 2020. https://www.spot.ph/arts-culture/the-latest-arts-culture/76169/parol-history-background-a2748-20181225-lfrm.

Tintiangco-Cubales, Allyson & Sacramento, Jocyl. Practicing Pinayist Pedagogy, *Amerasia Journal* 35, no.1 (2009). 179-187. DOI: 10.17953/amer.35.1.98257024r4501756.

REVOLUTION AND REVELATION

Brockell, Gillian. "Statue of Liberty was Created to Celebrate Freed Slaves not Immigrants." *The Washington Post*, May 23, 2019. Accessed July 20, 2020. https://www.washingtonpost.com/history/2019/05/23/statue-liberty-was-created-celebrate-freed-slaves-not-immigrants/.

Corazon de Jesus, Jose. "Bayan Ko." Translated by Philippine Study Group of Minnesota. *Crossroads Resource Center*. Accessed June 12, 2020. https://www.crcworks.org/bayanko.pdf.

Bughaw Organization Philippines. "LUMAD: Schools Under Attack." University of the Philippines. Streamed on YouTube April 23, 2018. YouTube video, 11:48. https://www.youtube.com/watch?v=A6syS5SZDVQ.

Discography of American Historical Recordings, s.v. "De Jesus, Jose Corazon." University of California, Santa Barbara, August 8, 1934. Accessed February 15, 2021. https://adp.library.ucsb.edu/index.php/matrix/detail/200017426/BS-83664-Bayan_ko.

King, Luther Martin Dr. "The Other America." Speech presented at Stanford University, Stanford, CA, April 4, 1967.

McClure, Tess. "Indigenous Human Rights Activists Face Targeting, Death in the Philippines." *Vice*, August 2, 2018. https://www.vice.com/en/article/qvmzed/indigenous-human-rights-activists-face-targeting-death-in-the-philippines.

Lazarus, Emma. "The New Colossus." Inscription carving. Statue of Liberty, New York NY, 1883.

Made in the USA
Monee, IL
14 November 2022

17728797R00098